THE YALE SHAKESPEARE

EDITED BY

WILBUR L. CROSS   TUCKER BROOKE

PUBLISHED UNDER THE DIRECTION
OF THE
DEPARTMENT OF ENGLISH, YALE UNIVERSITY,
ON THE FUND
GIVEN TO THE YALE UNIVERSITY PRESS IN 1917
BY THE MEMBERS OF THE
KINGSLEY TRUST ASSOCIATION
(SCROLL AND KEY SOCIETY OF YALE COLLEGE)
TO COMMEMORATE THE SEVENTY-FIFTH ANNIVERSARY
OF THE FOUNDING OF THE SOCIETY

·: *The Yale Shakespeare* :·

TWO GENTLEMEN OF VERONA

EDITED BY

KARL YOUNG

NEW HAVEN · YALE UNIVERSITY PRESS
LONDON · HUMPHREY MILFORD
OXFORD UNIVERSITY PRESS · MCMXXIV

TABLE OF CONTENTS

		PAGE
THE TEXT		1
NOTES		84
APPENDIX A.	Sources of the Play . .	90
APPENDIX B.	The History of the Play .	93
APPENDIX C.	The Text of the Present Edition	95
APPENDIX D.	Suggestions for Collateral Reading . . .	98
INDEX OF WORDS GLOSSED		99

The facsimile opposite reproduces the title-page of Bartholomew Yonge's translation (1598) of Montemayor's 'Diana.' The photograph was made from the copy of this book in the Yale University Library. The relation of Montemayor's 'Diana' to Shakespeare's play is discussed in Appendix A.

DIANA

of GEORGE OF MONTEMAYOR:

Translated out of Spanish into
English by BARTHOLOMEW
YONG *of the* Middle
Temple Gentleman.

At London.

Printed by Edm. Bollifant,
impensis G. B.

[DRAMATIS PERSONÆ]

THE NAMES OF ALL THE ACTORS

DUKE [of Milan], *father to Silvia*
VALENTINE, } *the two Gentlemen*
PROTEUS,
ANTONIO, *father to Proteus*
THURIO, *a foolish rival to Valentine*
EGLAMOUR, *agent for Silvia in her escape*
Host, *where Julia lodges* [in Milan]
Outlaws, *with Valentine*
SPEED, *a clownish servant to Valentine*
LAUNCE, *the like to Proteus*
PANTHINO, *servant to Antonio*

JULIA, *beloved of Proteus*
SILVIA, *beloved of Valentine*
LUCETTA, *waiting-woman to Julia*

[Servants, Musicians]

[SCENE: *Verona; Milan; and a forest on the frontier
of Mantua*]

Dramatis Personæ; *cf. n.*

The Two Gentlemen of Verona

ACT FIRST

Scene One

[*Verona.   An open place*]

[*Enter*] *Valentine* [*and*] *Proteus; and* [*later,*] *Speed.*

Val. Cease to persuade, my loving Proteus;
Home-keeping youth have ever homely wits.
Were 't not affection chains thy tender days
To the sweet glances of thy honour'd love,   **4**
I rather would entreat thy company
To see the wonders of the world abroad
Than, living dully sluggardiz'd at home,
Wear out thy youth with shapeless idleness.   **8**
But since thou lov'st, love still, and thrive therein,
Even as I would when I to love begin.
   Pro. Wilt thou be gone?   Sweet Valentine, adieu!
Think on thy Proteus, when thou haply seest   **12**
Some rare noteworthy object in thy travel.
Wish me partaker in thy happiness
When thou dost meet good hap; and in thy danger,
If ever danger do environ thee,   **16**
Commend thy grievance to my holy prayers,
For I will be thy beadsman, Valentine.
   Val. And on a love-book pray for my success?
   Pro. Upon some book I love I'll pray for thee.   **20**
   Val. That's on some shallow story of deep love,

8 shapeless: *aimless*   9 still: *always*   12 haply: *by chance*
17 Commend . . . to: *commit to the attention of*
18 beadsman: *one employed to pray for others*
19 love-book: *book treating of love (instead of prayer-book)*

How young Leander cross'd the Hellespont.

   Pro. That's a deep story of a deeper love;

For he was more than over shoes in love.   24

   Val. 'Tis true; for you are over boots in love,

And yet you never swum the Hellespont.

   Pro. Over the boots? nay, give me not the boots.

   Val. No, I will not, for it boots thee not.

   Pro.   What? 28

   Val. To be in love, where scorn is bought with
      groans;

Coy looks with heart-sore sighs; one fading moment's
      mirth

With twenty watchful, weary, tedious nights:

If haply won, perhaps a hapless gain;   32

If lost, why then a grievous labour won;

However, but a folly bought with wit,

Or else a wit by folly vanquished.

   Pro. So, by your circumstance, you call me fool. 36

   Val. So, by your circumstance, I fear you'll prove.

   Pro. 'Tis love you cavil at; I am not Love.

   Val. Love is your master, for he masters you;

And he that is so yoked by a fool,   40

Methinks, should not be chronicled for wise.

   Pro. Yet writers say, as in the sweetest bud

The eating canker dwells, so eating love

Inhabits in the finest wits of all.   44

   Val. And writers say, as the most forward bud

Is eaten by the canker ere it blow,

Even so by love the young and tender wit

Is turned to folly, blasting in the bud,   48

Losing his verdure even in the prime,

---

22 Leander; *cf. n.*   27 give . . . boots: *do not make game of me*
28 boots: *profits*   34 However: *in any case*
36 circumstance: *circumlocution*   37 circumstance: *state of affairs*
43 canker: *cankerworm*   44 Inhabits: *dwells*
46 blow: *bloom*   49 prime: *spring*

And all the fair effects of future hopes.
But wherefore waste I time to counsel thee
That art a votary to fond desire?   52
Once more adieu! my father at the road
Expects my coming, there to see me shipp'd.

   Pro. And thither will I bring thee, Valentine.

   Val. Sweet Proteus, no; now let us take our leave. 56
To Milan let me hear from thee by letters
Of thy success in love, and what news else
Betideth here in absence of thy friend;
And I likewise will visit thee with mine.   60

   Pro. All happiness bechance to thee in Milan!

   Val. As much to you at home! and so, farewell.

                              Exit.

   Pro. He after honour hunts, I after love.
He leaves his friends to dignify them more;   64
I leave myself, my friends, and all, for love.
Thou, Julia, thou hast metamorphos'd me;
Made me neglect my studies, lose my time,
War with good counsel, set the world at nought;   68
Made wit with musing weak, heart sick with thought.

              [Enter Speed.]

   Speed. Sir Proteus, save you! Saw you my master?

   Pro. But now he parted hence, to embark for Milan.

   Speed. Twenty to one, then, he is shipp'd already, 72
And I have play'd the sheep, in losing him.

   Pro. Indeed, a sheep doth very often stray,
An if the shepherd be a while away.

   Speed. You conclude that my master is a 76
shepherd, then, and I a sheep?

---

50 fair . . . hopes: *realization of hopes of future bliss*
52 fond: *foolish*   53 road: *anchorage*
54 shipp'd; *cf. n.*   55 bring: *accompany*
58 success: *fortune (good or bad)*   69 thought: *sorrow*
72, 73 shipp'd . . . sheep; *cf. n.*   75 An if: *if*

Pro. I do.

Speed. Why then my horns are his horns, whether I wake or sleep.   80

Pro. A silly answer, and fitting well a sheep.

Speed. This proves me still a sheep.

Pro. True, and thy master a shepherd.

Speed. Nay, that I can deny by a circum- 84 stance.

Pro. It shall go hard but I'll prove it by another.

Speed. The shepherd seeks the sheep, and 88 not the sheep the shepherd; but I seek my master, and my master seeks not me: therefore I am no sheep.

Pro. The sheep for fodder follow the shep- 92 herd, the shepherd for food follows not the sheep; thou for wages followest thy master, thy master for wages follows not thee: therefore thou art a sheep.   96

Speed. Such another proof will make me cry 'baa.'

Pro. But, dost thou hear? gavest thou my letter to Julia?   100

Speed. Ay, sir; I, a lost mutton, gave your letter to her, a laced mutton; and she, a laced mutton, gave me, a lost mutton, nothing for my labour.   104

Pro. Here's too small a pasture for such store of muttons.

Speed. If the ground be overcharged, you were best stick her.   108

79 horns: *fancifully attributed to cuckolds*
84 circumstance: *detailed proof*   98 'baa': *quibble on 'bah'*
102 laced mutton: *courtesan; cf. n.*
107 overcharged: *overburdened*   108 stick: *stab*

   Pro. Nay, in that you are astray; 'twere best pound you.

   Speed. Nay, sir, less than a pound shall serve me for carrying your letter.   112

   Pro. You mistake; I mean the pound,—a pinfold.

   Speed. From a pound to a pin? Fold it over and over,

'Tis threefold too little for carrying a letter to your 116 lover.

   Pro. But what said she?

   Speed. [*Nodding.*] Ay.

   Pro. Nod, ay? why, that's noddy.   120

   Speed. You mistook, sir. I say she did nod; and you ask me if she did nod; and I say, 'Ay.'

   Pro. And that set together is—noddy.

   Speed. Now you have taken the pains to set 124 it together, take it for your pains.

   Pro. No, no; you shall have it for bearing the letter.

   Speed. Well, I perceive I must be fain to bear 128 with you.

   Pro. Why, sir, how do you bear with me?

   Speed. Marry, sir, the letter very orderly; having nothing but the word 'noddy' for my 132 pains.

   Pro. Beshrew me, but you have a quick wit.

   Speed. And yet it cannot overtake your slow purse.   136

   Pro. Come, come; open the matter in brief. What said she?

110 pound: *confine within an enclosure (with quibble)*
114 pinfold: *enclosure for stray animals*   120 noddy: *simpleton*
128 fain: *pleased*   131 Marry: *by the Virgin Mary; cf. n.*
134 Beshrew: *curse (used playfully)*   137 open: *disclose*

Speed. Open your purse, that the money and
the matter may be both at once delivered. 140

Pro. Well, sir, here is for your pains [*giving
him money*]. What said she?

Speed. Truly, sir, I think you'll hardly win her.

Pro. Why, couldst thou perceive so much 144
from her?

Speed. Sir, I could perceive nothing at all
from her; no, not so much as a ducat for
delivering your letter. And being so hard to 148
me that brought your mind, I fear she'll prove
as hard to you in telling your mind. Give her
no token but stones, for she's as hard as steel.

Pro. What! said she nothing? 152

Speed. No, not so much as 'Take this for
thy pains.' To testify your bounty, I thank you,
you have testerned me; in requital whereof,
henceforth carry your letters yourself. And so, 156
sir, I'll commend you to my master.

Pro. Go, go, be gone, to save your ship from wrack;
Which cannot perish, having thee aboard,
Being destin'd to a drier death on shore.— 160

[*Exit Speed.*]

I must go send some better messenger.
I fear my Julia would not deign my lines,
Receiving them from such a worthless post. *Exit.*

146 perceive: *receive*   147 ducat: *a gold or silver coin*
150 in telling: *when you tell her*   151 stones: *jewels (possibly)*
155 testerned: *'tipped' with a tester, or sixpence*
160 destin'd . . . shore; *cf. n.*   162 deign: *accept graciously*
163 post: *messenger (with quibble)*

Scene Two

[*The Same. The Garden of Julia's House*]

Enter Julia and Lucetta.

Jul. But say, Lucetta, now we are alone,
Wouldst thou then counsel me to fall in love?

Luc. Ay, madam, so you stumble not unheedfully.

Jul. Of all the fair resort of gentlemen   4
That every day with parle encounter me,
In thy opinion which is worthiest love?

Luc. Please you repeat their names, I'll show my
    mind
According to my shallow simple skill.   8

Jul. What think'st thou of the fair Sir Eglamour?

Luc. As of a knight well-spoken, neat and fine;
But, were I you, he never should be mine.

Jul. What think'st thou of the rich Mercatio?   12

Luc. Well of his wealth; but of himself, so so.

Jul. What think'st thou of the gentle Proteus?

Luc. Lord, Lord! to see what folly reigns in us!

Jul. How now! what means this passion at his
    name?   16

Luc. Pardon, dear madam; 'tis a passing shame
That I, unworthy body as I am,
Should censure thus on lovely gentlemen.

Jul. Why not on Proteus, as of all the rest?   20

Luc. Then thus: of many good I think him best.

Jul. Your reason?

Luc. I have no other but a woman's reason:
I think him so because I think him so.   24

Jul. And wouldst thou have me cast my love on him?

---

4 resort: *gathering*   5 parle: *conversation*
9 Sir Eglamour; *cf. n.*   17 passing: *surpassing*
19 censure: *pass judgment*

Luc. Ay, if you thought your love not cast away.

Jul. Why, he of all the rest hath never mov'd me.

Luc. Yet he of all the rest, I think, best loves ye.   28

Jul. His little speaking shows his love but small.

Luc. Fire that's closest kept burns most of all.

Jul. They do not love that do not show their love.

Luc. O! they love least that let men know their love.   32

Jul. I would I knew his mind.

Luc.   Peruse this paper, madam.
                              [*Gives a letter.*]

Jul. 'To Julia.'—Say from whom?

Luc.   That the contents will show.

Jul. Say, say, who gave it thee?

Luc. Sir Valentine's page, and sent, I think, from Proteus.   36

He would have given it you, but I, being in the way,

Did in your name receive it.   Pardon the fault, I pray.

Jul. Now, by my modesty, a goodly broker!

Dare you presume to harbour wanton lines?   40

To whisper and conspire against my youth?

Now, trust me, 'tis an office of great worth,

And you an officer fit for the place.

There, take the paper; see it be return'd;   44

Or else return no more into my sight.

Luc. To plead for love deserves more fee than hate.

Jul. Will ye be gone?

Luc.   That you may ruminate.   *Exit.*

Jul. And yet I would I had o'erlook'd the letter.   48

It were a shame to call her back again

And pray her to a fault for which I chid her.

What 'fool is she, that knows I am a maid,

And would not force the letter to my view!   52

27 mov'd: *made a proposal to*   39 broker: *go-between*
48 o'erlook'd: *looked over, read*   51 'fool: *a fool*

Since maids, in modesty, say 'No' to that
Which they would have the profferer construe 'Ay.'
Fie, fie! how wayward is this foolish love
That, like a testy babe, will scratch the nurse   56
And presently all humbled kiss the rod!
How churlishly I chid Lucetta hence,
When willingly I would have had her here!
How angerly I taught my brow to frown,   60
When inward joy enforc'd my heart to smile!
My penance is, to call Lucetta back
And ask remission for my folly past.
What ho! Lucetta!

[Enter Lucetta.]

Luc.   What would your ladyship?   64
Jul. Is it near dinner-time?
Luc.   I would it were,
That you might kill your stomach on your meat,
And not upon your maid.
Jul. What is 't that you took up so gingerly?   68
Luc. Nothing.
Jul. Why didst thou stoop, then?
Luc.   To take a paper up
That I let fall.
Jul.   And is that paper nothing?
Luc. Nothing concerning me.   72
Jul. Then let it lie for those that it concerns.
Luc. Madam, it will not lie where it concerns,
Unless it have a false interpreter.
Jul. Some love of yours hath writ to you in rime.   76
Luc. That I might sing it, madam, to a tune.
Give me a note; your ladyship can set.

56 testy: *fretful*   57 presently: *immediately*
60 angerly: *angrily*   66 kill: *i.e. subdue, satisfy*   stomach; *cf. n.*
66, 67 meat . . . maid; *cf. n.*   74 concerns: *is of importance*
78 set; *cf. n.*

Jul. As little by such toys as may be possible;
Best sing it to the tune of 'Light o' Love.'   80
    Luc. It is too heavy for so light a tune.
    Jul. Heavy! belike it hath some burden, then?
    Luc. Ay; and melodious were it, would you sing it.
    Jul. And why not you?
    Luc.   I cannot reach so high. 84
    Jul. Let's see your song. [*Taking the letter.*] How
        now, minion!
    Luc. Keep tune there still, so you will sing it out.
And yet, methinks, I do not like this tune.
    Jul. You do not?
    Luc.   No, madam; it is too sharp. 88
    Jul. You, minion, are too saucy.
    Luc. Nay, now you are too flat,
And mar the concord with too harsh a descant.
There wanteth but a mean to fill your song.   92
    Jul. The mean is drown'd with your unruly bass.
    Luc. Indeed, I bid the base for Proteus.
    Jul. This babble shall not henceforth trouble me.
Here is a coil with protestation!—   96
                              [*Tears the letter.*]
Go, get you gone, and let the papers lie:
You would be fingering them, to anger me.
    Luc. She makes it strange; but she would be best
        pleas'd
To be so anger'd with another letter.   [*Exit.*] 100
    Jul. Nay, would I were so anger'd with the same!
O hateful hands, to tear such loving words!
Injurious wasps, to feed on such sweet honey,

80 'Light o' Love': *name of a tune then familiar*
81 heavy: *serious*   82 burden; *cf. n.*
90 flat; *cf. n.*   91, 92 descant . . . mean; *cf. n.*
94 bid the base; *cf. n.*
96 coil with protestation: *turmoil over solemn declaration*
99 makes it strange: *pretends aloofness*
101 would . . . same; *cf. n.*   103 wasps: *i.e. her fingers*

And kill the bees that yield it with your stings!   104
I'll kiss each several paper for amends.
Look, here is writ 'kind Julia.'   Unkind Julia!
As in revenge of thy ingratitude,
I throw thy name against the bruising stones,   108
Trampling contemptuously on thy disdain.
And here is writ 'love-wounded Proteus.'
Poor wounded name! my bosom as a bed
Shall lodge thee till thy wound be throughly
     heal'd;   112
And thus I search it with a sovereign kiss.
But twice or thrice was 'Proteus' written down.
Be calm, good wind, blow not a word away
Till I have found each letter in the letter,   116
Except mine own name; that some whirlwind bear
Unto a ragged, fearful hanging rock,
And throw it thence into the raging sea!
Lo! here in one line is his name twice writ,   120
'Poor forlorn Proteus, passionate Proteus,
To the sweet Julia.'   That I'll tear away;
And yet I will not, sith so prettily
He couples it to his complaining names.   124
Thus will I fold them one upon another.
Now kiss, embrace, contend, do what you will.

[Enter Lucetta.]

   Luc. Madam,
Dinner is ready, and your father stays.   128
   Jul. Well, let us go.
   Luc. What! shall these papers lie like telltales here?
   Jul. If you respect them, best to take them up.
   Luc. Nay, I was taken up for laying them down;   132

107 As: *thus*
113 search: *probe, cleanse*
131 respect: *prize*
112 throughly: *thoroughly*
128 stays: *waits*
132 taken up: *rebuked*

Yet here they shall not lie, for catching cold.

Jul. I see you have a month's mind to them.

Luc. Ay, madam, you may say what sights you see;
I see things too, although you judge I wink.   136

Jul. Come, come; will 't please you go?   *Exeunt.*

Scene Three

[*The Same.   A Room in Antonio's House*]

Enter Antonio and Panthino; [and later,] Proteus.

Ant. Tell me, Panthino, what sad talk was that
Wherewith my brother held you in the cloister?

Pant. 'Twas of his nephew Proteus, your son.

Ant. Why, what of him?

Pant.   He wonder'd that your lordship   4
Would suffer him to spend his youth at home,
While other men, of slender reputation,
Put forth their sons to seek preferment out:
Some to the wars, to try their fortune there;   8
Some to discover islands far away;
Some to the studious universities.
For any or for all these exercises
He said that Proteus your son was meet,   12
And did request me to importune you
To let him spend his time no more at home,
Which would be great impeachment to his age,
In having known no travel in his youth.   16

Ant. Nor need'st thou much importune me to that
Whereon this month I have been hammering.
I have consider'd well his loss of time,
And how he cannot be a perfect man,   20

133 for: *for fear of*
136 wink: *close the eyes*
13 importune: *urge*
18 hammering: *planning*

134 month's mind: *strong inclination*
1 sad: *serious*
15 impeachment: *reproach*

Not being tried and tutor'd in the world.
Experience is by industry achiev'd,
And perfected by the swift course of time.
Then tell me, whither were I best to send him?   24
    Pant. I think your lordship is not ignorant
How his companion, youthful Valentine,
Attends the emperor in his royal court.
    Ant. I know it well.   28
    Pant. 'Twere good, I think, your lordship sent him
        thither.
There shall he practise tilts and tournaments,
Hear sweet discourse, converse with noblemen,
And be in eye of every exercise   32
Worthy his youth and nobleness of birth.
    Ant. I like thy counsel; well hast thou advis'd;
And that thou mayst perceive how well I like it,
The execution of it shall make known.   36
Even with the speediest expedition
I will dispatch him to the emperor's court.
    Pant. To-morrow, may it please you, Don Alphonso
With other gentlemen of good esteem   40
Are journeying to salute the emperor,
And to commend their service to his will.
    Ant. Good company; with them shall Proteus go,
And—in good time! Now will we break with him.   44

[*Enter Proteus.*]

    Pro. Sweet love! sweet lines! sweet life!
Here is her hand, the agent of her heart;
Here is her oath for love, her honour's pawn.
O that our fathers would applaud our loves,   48
To seal our happiness with their consents!

27 emperor; *cf. n.*   32 be in eye of: *have opportunity of seeing*
42 commend: *commit*   44 in good time; *cf n.*
44 break with: *disclose our purpose to*   47 pawn: *pledge*

O heavenly Julia!

    Ant. How now! what letter are you reading there?

    Pro. May't please your lordship, 'tis a word or
two   52

Of commendations sent from Valentine,

Deliver'd by a friend that came from him.

    Ant. Lend me the letter; let me see what news.

    Pro. There is no news, my lord; but that he writes 56

How happily he lives, how well belov'd

And daily graced by the emperor;

Wishing me with him, partner of his fortune.

    Ant. And how stand you affected to his wish?   60

    Pro. As one relying on your lordship's will

And not depending on his friendly wish.

    Ant. My will is something sorted with his wish.

Muse not that I thus suddenly proceed;   64

For what I will, I will, and there an end.

I am resolv'd that thou shalt spend some time

With Valentinus in the emperor's court.

What maintenance he from his friends receives,   68

Like exhibition thou shalt have from me.

To-morrow be in readiness to go.

Excuse it not, for I am peremptory.

    Pro. My lord, I cannot be so soon provided.   72

Please you, deliberate a day or two.

    Ant. Look, what thou want'st shall be sent after
thee.

No more of stay; to-morrow thou must go.

Come on, Panthino; you shall be employ'd   76

To hasten on his expedition.

                  [Exeunt Antonio and Panthino.]

---

53 commendations: *greetings*   58 graced: *honored*
63 something sorted: *rather in agreement*
64 Muse: *grumble*   69 exhibition: *allowance of money*
71 Excuse: *beg off from*   peremptory: *determined*
72 provided: *equipped*

Pro. Thus have I shunn'd the fire for fear of burn-
   ing,
And drench'd me in the sea, where I am drown'd.
I fear'd to show my father Julia's letter,   80
Lest he should take exceptions to my love;
And with the vantage of mine own excuse
Hath he excepted most against my love.
O! how this spring of love resembleth   84
   The uncertain glory of an April day,
Which now shows all the beauty of the sun,
   And by and by a cloud takes all away!

[*Enter Panthino.*]

Pant. Sir Proteus, your father calls for you.   88
He is in haste; therefore, I pray you, go.
   Pro. Why, this it is: my heart accords thereto,
And yet a thousand times it answers, 'no.'   *Exeunt.*

ACT SECOND

Scene One

[*Milan.   A Room in the Duke's Palace*]

Enter Valentine [*and*] *Speed;* [*and later,*] *Silvia.*

Speed. Sir, your glove.   [*Offering a glove.*]
Val.   Not mine; my gloves are on.
Speed. Why, then this may be yours, for this is but
   one.
   Val. Ha! let me see: ay, give it me, it's mine;
Sweet ornament that decks a thing divine!   4
Ah Silvia! Silvia!

81 take exceptions: *make objections*
83 excepted . . . against: *objected to*   1, 2 on . . . one; *cf. n.*

Speed. [*Calling.*] Madam Silvia! Madam Silvia!

Val. How now, sirrah?　　　　　　　　　8

Speed. She is not within hearing, sir.

Val. Why, sir, who bade you call her?

Speed. Your worship, sir; or else I mistook.

Val. Well, you'll still be too forward.　　12

Speed. And yet I was last chidden for being too slow.

Val. Go to, sir. Tell me, do you know Madam Silvia?　　　　　　　　　16

Speed. She that your worship loves?

Val. Why, how know you that I am in love?

Speed. Marry, by these special marks: first, you have learned, like Sir Proteus, to wreathe 20 your arms, like a malcontent; to relish a love-song, like a robin-redbreast; to walk alone, like one that had the pestilence; to sigh, like a schoolboy that had lost his A B C; to weep, like 24 a young wench that had buried her grandam; to fast, like one that takes diet; to watch, like one that fears robbing; to speak puling, like a beggar at Hallowmas. You were wont, when 28 you laughed, to crow like a cock; when you walked, to walk like one of the lions; when you fasted, it was presently after dinner; when you looked sadly, it was for want of money; and now 32 you are metamorphosed with a mistress, that, when I look on you, I can hardly think you my master.

8 sirrah: *form of address to inferiors*
15 Go to: *an expression of disapprobation*
21 relish: *sing*
26 watch: *lie awake, or sit up at night*
28 Hallowmas; *cf. n.*
33 that: *so that*

20 wreathe: *fold*
24 A B C: *primer*
27 puling: *whiningly*
30 one . . . lions; *cf. n.*

Val. Are all these things perceived in me?   36

Speed. They are all perceived without ye.

Val. Without me? they cannot.

Speed. Without you? nay, that's certain; for, without you were so simple, none else would; 40 but you are so without these follies, that these follies are within you and shine through you like the water in an urinal, that not an eye that sees you but is a physician to comment on your 44 malady.

Val. But tell me, dost thou know my lady Silvia?

Speed. She that you gaze on so as she sits at 48 supper?

Val. Hast thou observed that? even she, I mean.

Speed. Why, sir, I know her not.   52

Val. Dost thou know her by my gazing on her, and yet knowest her not?

Speed. Is she not hard-favoured, sir?

Val. Not so fair, boy, as well-favoured.   56

Speed. Sir, I know that well enough.

Val. What dost thou know?

Speed. That she is not so fair, as, of you, well-favoured.   60

Val. I mean that her beauty is exquisite, but her favour infinite.

Speed. That's because the one is painted and the other out of all count.   64

Val. How painted? and how out of count?

40 would: *i.e. would perceive them*
43 urinal: *transparent receptacle for testing urine*
55 hard-favoured: *ugly*   56 well-favoured: *charming*
62 favour: *charm*

Speed. Marry, sir, so painted to make her fair, that no man counts of her beauty.

Val. How esteemest thou me? I account of 68 her beauty.

Speed. You never saw her since she was deformed.

Val. How long hath she been deformed?   72

Speed. Ever since you loved her.

Val. I have loved her ever since I saw her, and still I see her beautiful.

Speed. If you love her, you cannot see her.   76

Val. Why?

Speed. Because Love is blind. O! that you had mine eyes; or your own eyes had the lights they were wont to have when you chid at Sir 80 Proteus for going ungartered!

Val. What should I see then?

Speed. Your own present folly and her passing deformity: for he, being in love, could not 84 see to garter his hose; and you, being in love, cannot see to put on your hose.

Val. Belike, boy, then, you are in love; for last morning you could not see to wipe my 88 shoes.

Speed. True, sir; I was in love with my bed. I thank you, you swinged me for my love, which makes me the bolder to chide you for 92 yours.

Val. In conclusion, I stand affected to her.

Speed. I would you were set, so your affection would cease.   96

67 counts of: *takes account of*
81 going ungartered: *a convention of love-sickness*
91 swinged: *beat*   95 set: *seated*

Val. Last night she enjoined me to write some lines to one she loves.

Speed. And have you?

Val. I have.   100

Speed. Are they not lamely writ?

Val. No, boy, but as well as I can do them. Peace! here she comes.

[*Enter Silvia.*]

Speed. [*Aside.*] O excellent motion! O ex- 104 ceeding puppet! Now will he interpret to her.

Val. Madam and mistress, a thousand good morrows.

Speed. [*Aside.*] O! 'give ye good even: here's 108 a million of manners.

Sil. Sir Valentine and servant, to you two thousand.

Speed. [*Aside.*] He should give her interest, 112 and she gives it him.

Val. As you enjoin'd me, I have writ your letter
Unto the secret nameless friend of yours;
Which I was much unwilling to proceed in 116
But for my duty to your ladyship.   [*Gives a letter.*]

Sil. I thank you, gentle servant. 'Tis very clerkly done.

Val. Now trust me, madam, it came hardly off; 120
For, being ignorant to whom it goes
I writ at random, very doubtfully.

Sil. Perchance you think too much of so much pains?

Val. No, madam; so it stead you, I will write, 124
Please you command, a thousand times as much.

104, 105 motion . . . puppet . . . interpret; *cf. n.*
108 'give: *God give*   110 servant; *cf. n.*
119 clerkly: *in a scholarly manner*   124 stead: *benefit*

And yet—

Sil. A pretty period! Well, I guess the sequel;
And yet I will not name it; and yet I care not;   128
And yet take this again; and yet I thank you,
Meaning henceforth to trouble you no more.

Speed. [*Aside.*] And yet you will; and yet another
    'yet.'

Val. What means your ladyship? do you not like
    it?   132

Sil. Yes, yes: the lines are very quaintly writ;
But since unwillingly, take them again.
Nay, take them.   [*Gives back the letter.*]

Val.   Madam, they are for you.

Sil. Ay, ay; you writ them, sir, at my request,   136
But I will none of them; they are for you.
I would have had them writ more movingly.

Val. Please you, I'll write your ladyship another.

Sil. And when it's writ, for my'sake read it over;   140
And if it please you, so; if not, why, so.

Val. If it please me, madam, what then?

Sil. Why, if it please you, take it for your labour;
And so, good morrow, servant.   *Exit Silvia.*   144

Speed. O jest unseen, inscrutable, invisible,
As a nose on a man's face, or a weathercock on a
    steeple!
My master sues to her, and she hath taught her suitor,
He being her pupil, to become her tutor.   148
O excellent device! was there ever heard a better,
That my master, being scribe, to himself should write
    the letter?

Val. How now, sir! what are you reasoning with
    yourself?

127 period: *full pause*   129 again: *back*
133 quaintly: *skilfully*   151 reasoning: *talking of*

Speed. Nay, I was riming; 'tis you that have the
   reason.   152

Val. To do what?

Speed. To be a spokesman from Madam Silvia.

Val. To whom?

Speed. To yourself. Why, she wooes you by a
   figure.   156

Val. What figure?

Speed. By a letter, I should say.

Val. Why, she hath not writ to me?

Speed. What need she, when she hath made 160
you write to yourself? Why, do you not perceive
the jest?

Val. No, believe me.

Speed. No believing you, indeed, sir. But did 164
you perceive her earnest?

Val. She gave me none, except an angry word.

Speed. Why, she hath given you a letter.

Val. That's the letter I writ to her friend.   168

Speed. And that letter hath she delivered, and
there an end.

Val. I would it were no worse.

Speed. I'll warrant you, 'tis as well: 172
'For often have you writ to her, and she, in modesty,
Or else for want of idle time, could not again reply;
Or fearing else some messenger that might her mind
   discover,
Herself hath taught her love himself to write unto her
   lover.'   176
All this I speak in print, for in print I found it.
Why muse you, sir? 'Tis dinner-time.

Val. I have dined.

156 by a figure: *indirectly*   165, 166 earnest . . . none; *cf. n.*
174 again reply: *reply*   177 speak in print: *speak precisely; cf. n.*
179 dined: *i.e. feasted on the sight of Silvia*

Speed. Ay, but hearken, sir. Though the 180
chameleon Love can feed on the air, I am one
that am nourished by my victuals, and would
fain have meat. O! be not like your mistress;
be moved, be moved.   *Exeunt.*

Scene Two

[*Verona.   A Room in Julia's House*]

Enter Proteus [and] Julia; [and later,] Panthino.

Pro. Have patience, gentle Julia.
Jul. I must, where is no remedy.
Pro. When possibly I can, I will return.
Jul. If you turn not, you will return the sooner.   4
Keep this remembrance for thy Julia's sake.
                          [*Gives him a ring.*]
Pro. Why, then, we'll make exchange. Here, take
   you this.   [*Gives her another.*]
Jul. And seal the bargain with a holy kiss.
Pro. Here is my hand for my true constancy;   8
And when that hour o'erslips me in the day
Wherein I sigh not, Julia, for thy sake,
The next ensuing hour some foul mischance
Torment me for my love's forgetfulness!   12
My father stays my coming; answer not.
The tide is now,—nay, not thy tide of tears;
That tide will stay me longer than I should.
Julia, farewell.   [*Exit Julia.*]
                  What! gone without a word?   16
Ay, so true love should do; it cannot speak;
For truth hath better deeds than words to grace it.

4 turn: *change, prove unfaithful*   14 tide; *cf. n. on* I. i. 54

[*Enter Panthino.*]

Pant. Sir Proteus, you are stay'd for.

Pro.   Go; I come, I come.
Alas! this parting strikes poor lovers dumb.   20
                                        Exeunt.

Scene Three

[*The Same.   A Street*]

*Enter Launce, [leading a dog; and later enter]
Panthino.*

Launce. Nay, 'twill be this hour ere I have done
weeping; all the kind of the Launces have this
very fault. I have received my proportion, like the
prodigious son, and am going with Sir Proteus 4
to the imperial's court. I think Crab my dog be
the sourest-natured dog that lives. My mother
weeping, my father wailing, my sister crying, our
maid howling, our cat wringing her hands, and 8
all our house in a great perplexity, yet did not
this cruel-hearted cur shed one tear. He is a
stone, a very pebble stone, and has no more pity
in him than a dog. A Jew would have wept to 12
have seen our parting; why, my grandam, having no eyes, look you, wept herself blind at my
parting. Nay, I'll show you the manner of it.
This shoe is my father; no, this left shoe is my 16
father; no, no, this left shoe is my mother;
nay, that cannot be so neither; yes, it is so; it
is so; it hath the worser sole. This shoe, with
the hole in it, is my mother, and this my father. A 20

2 kind: *family, kindred*
3, 4 proportion, prodigious: *malapropisms for 'portion' and 'prodigal'*
5 imperial's: *emperor's*

vengeance on 't! there 'tis. Now, sir, this staff is
my sister; for, look you, she is as white as a lily
and as small as a wand. This hat is Nan, our
maid. I am the dog; no, the dog is himself, and 24
I am the dog,—O! the dog is me, and I am myself; ay, so, so. Now come I to my father: 'Father, your blessing.' Now should not the shoe
speak a word for weeping. Now should I kiss my 28
father; well, he weeps on. Now come I to my
mother. O, that she could speak now like a
wood woman! Well, I kiss her; why, there 'tis;
here's my mother's breath up and down. Now 32
come I to my sister; mark the moan she makes.
Now the dog all this while sheds not a tear nor
speaks a word; but see how I lay the dust with
my tears.   36

[*Enter Panthino.*]

Pant. Launce, away, away, aboard! Thy master is shipped, and thou art to post after with
oars. What's the matter? why weepest thou,
man? Away, ass! you'll lose the tide if you tarry 40
any longer.

Launce. It is no matter if the tied were lost;
for it is the unkindest tied that ever any man tied.

Pant. What's the unkindest tide?   44

Launce. Why, he that's tied here, Crab, my
dog.

Pant. Tut, man, I mean thou'lt lose the
flood; and, in losing the flood, lose thy voyage, 48
and, in losing thy voyage, lose thy master; and,
in losing thy master, lose thy service; and, in

31 wood: *mad, distracted; cf. n.*   32 up and down: *exactly*
40 tide; *cf. n. on I. i. 54*

losing thy service,—Why dost thou stop my
mouth?   52

Launce. For fear thou shouldst lose thy
tongue.

Pant. Where should I lose my tongue?

Launce. In thy tale.   56

Pant. In thy tail!

Launce. Lose the tide, and the voyage, and
the master, and the service, and the tied! Why,
man, if the river were dry, I am able to fill it 60
with my tears; if the wind were down, I could
drive the boat with my sighs.

Pant. Come, come away, man; I was sent to
call thee.   64

Launce. Sir, call me what thou darest.

Pant. Wilt thou go?

Launce. Well, I will go.   *Exeunt.*

Scene Four

[*Milan. A Room in the Duke's Palace*]

*Enter Valentine, Silvia, Thurio, [and] Speed; [and
later,] Duke [and] Proteus.*

Sil. Servant!

Val. Mistress?

Speed. Master, Sir Thurio frowns on you.

Val. Ay, boy, it's for love.   4

Speed. Not of you.

Val. Of my mistress, then.

Speed. 'Twere good you knock'd him.   [*Exit.*]

Sil. Servant, you are sad.   8

Val. Indeed, madam, I seem so.

Thu. Seem you that you are not?

Val. Haply I do.

Thu. So do counterfeits.   12

Val. So do you.

Thu. What seem I that I am not?

Val. Wise.

Thu. What instance of the contrary?   16

Val. Your folly.

Thu. And how quote you my folly?

Val. I quote it in your jerkin.

Thu. My jerkin is a doublet.   20

Val. Well, then, I'll double your folly.

Thu. How?

Sil. What, angry, Sir Thurio! do you change
colour?   24

Val. Give him leave, madam; he is a kind of
chameleon.

Thu. That hath more mind to feed on your
blood than live in your air.   28

Val. You have said, sir.

Thu. Ay, sir, and done too, for this time.

Val. I know it well, sir: you always end ere
you begin.   32

Sil. A fine volley of words, gentlemen, and
quickly shot off.

Val. 'Tis indeed, madam; we thank the
giver.   36

Sil. Who is that, servant?

Val. Yourself, sweet lady; for you gave the
fire. Sir Thurio borrows his wit from your ladyship's looks, and spends what he borrows kindly 40
in your company.

Thu. Sir, if you spend word for word with me,
I shall make your wit bankrupt.

18 quote: *observe; cf. n.*   20 jerkin, doublet; *cf. n.*
28 live . . . air; *cf. n.*

Val. I know it well, sir: you have an ex- 44
chequer of words, and, I think, no other treasure
to give your followers; for it appears by their
bare liveries that they live by your bare words.

Sil. No more, gentlemen, no more.   Here 48
comes my father.

[*Enter Duke.*]

Duke. Now, daughter Silvia, you are hard beset.
Sir Valentine, your father's in good health:
What say you to a letter from your friends   52
Of much good news?

Val.   My lord, I will be thankful
To any happy messenger from thence.

Duke. Know ye Don Antonio, your countryman?

Val. Ay, my good lord; I know the gentleman   56
To be of worth and worthy estimation,
And not without desert so well reputed.

Duke. Hath he not a son?

Val. Ay, my good lord; a son that well deserves   60
The honour and regard of such a father.

Duke. You know him well?

Val. I know him as myself; for from our infancy
We have convers'd and spent our hours together;   64
And though myself have been an idle truant,
Omitting the sweet benefit of time
To clothe mine age with angel-like perfection,
Yet hath Sir Proteus,—for that's his name,—   68
Made use and fair advantage of his days;
His years but young, but his experience old;
His head unmellow'd, but his judgment ripe;
And, in a word,—for far behind his worth   72

54 happy messenger: *bearer of good news*
64 convers'd: *been companions*   66 Omitting: *disregarding*
71 unmellow'd: *untinged with grey*

(

Come all the praises that I now bestow,—
He is complete in feature and in mind
With all good grace to grace a gentleman.

   Duke. Beshrew me, sir, but if he make this good, 76
He is as worthy for an empress' love
As meet to be an emperor's counsellor.
Well, sir, this gentleman is come to me
With commendation from great potentates;   80
And here he means to spend his time awhile.
I think, 'tis no unwelcome news to you.

   Val. Should I have wish'd a thing, it had been he.

   Duke. Welcome him then according to his worth. 84
Silvia, I speak to you; and you, Sir Thurio;
For Valentine, I need not cite him to it.
I'll send him hither to you presently.   *[Exit.]*

   Val. This is the gentleman I told your ladyship 88
Had come along with me, but that his mistress
Did hold his eyes lock'd in her crystal looks.

   Sil. Belike that now she hath enfranchis'd them
Upon some other pawn for fealty.   92

   Val. Nay, sure, I think she holds them prisoners
     still.

   Sil. Nay, then he should be blind; and, being blind,
How could he see his way to seek out you?

   Val. Why, lady, Love hath twenty pair of eyes. 96

   Thu. They say that Love hath not an eye at all.

   Val. To see such lovers, Thurio, as yourself.
Upon a homely object Love can wink.

   Sil. Have done, have done. Here comes the gentle-
     man.   *[Exit Thurio.]* 100

[Enter Proteus.]

---

74 feature: *outward form*   86 cite: *urge*
90 lock'd . . . looks; *cf. n.*
91 Belike: *'tis likely*   enfranchis'd: *released from confinement*

Val. Welcome, dear Proteus! Mistress, I beseech
    you,
Confirm his welcome with some special favour.

Sil. His worth is warrant for his welcome hither,
If this be he you oft have wish'd to hear from.   104

Val. Mistress, it is. Sweet lady, entertain him
To be my fellow-servant to your ladyship.

Sil. Too low a mistress for so high a servant.

Pro. Not so, sweet lady; but too mean a servant 108
To have a look of such a worthy mistress.

Val. Leave off discourse of disability.
Sweet lady, entertain him for your servant.

Pro. My duty will I boast of, nothing else.   112

Sil. And duty never yet did want his meed.
Servant, you are welcome to a worthless mistress.

Pro. I'll die on him that says so but yourself.

Sil. That you are welcome?

Pro.   That you are worthless. 116

[*Enter Thurio.*]

Thu. Madam, my lord your father would speak
    with you.

Sil. I wait upon his pleasure. Come, Sir Thurio,
Go with me. Once more, new servant, welcome.
I'll leave you to confer of home-affairs;   120
When you have done, we look to hear from you.

Pro. We'll both attend upon your ladyship.

                          [*Exeunt Silvia and Thurio.*]

Val. Now, tell me, how do all from whence you
    came?

Pro. Your friends are well and have them much
    commended.   124

---

105 entertain: *take into service*   113 meed:*'reward*
115 die on: *die in fight with*
124 them much commended: *sent kind remembrances*

Val. And how do yours?

Pro.   I left them all in health.

Val. How does your lady, and how thrives your
   love?

Pro. My tales of love were wont to weary you;
I know you joy not in a love-discourse.   128

Val. Ay, Proteus, but that life is alter'd now.
I have done penance for contemning love;
Whose high imperious thoughts have punish'd me
With bitter fasts, with penitential groans,   132
With nightly tears and daily heart-sore sighs;
For, in revenge of my contempt of love,
Love hath chas'd sleep from my enthralled eyes,
And made them watchers of mine own heart's sor-
   row.   136
O, gentle Proteus! Love's a mighty lord,
And hath so humbled me as I confess
There is no woe to his correction,
Nor to his service no such joy on earth.   140
Now no discourse, except it be of love;
Now can I break my fast, dine, sup, and sleep,
Upon the very naked name of love.

Pro. Enough; I read your fortune in your eye.   144
Was this the idol that you worship so?

Val. Even she; and is she not a heavenly saint?

Pro. No; but she is an earthly paragon.

Val. Call her divine.

Pro.   I will not flatter her.   148

Val. O! flatter me, for love delights in praises.

Pro. When I was sick, you gave me bitter pills,
And I must minister the like to you.

Val. Then speak the truth by her; if not divine,   152
Yet let her be a principality,

139 to: *comparable to*   153 principality; *cf. n.*

Sovereign to all the creatures on the earth
   Pro. Except my mistress.
   Val.   Sweet, except not any,
Except thou wilt except against my love.   156
   Pro. Have I not reason to prefer mine own?
   Val. And I will help thee to prefer her too.
She shall be dignified with this high honour,—
To bear my lady's train, lest the base earth   160
Should from her vesture chance to steal a kiss,
And, of so great a favour growing proud,
Disdain to root the summer-swelling flower,
And make rough winter everlastingly.   164
   Pro. Why, Valentine, what braggardism is this?
   Val. Pardon me, Proteus; all I can is nothing
To her whose worth makes other worthies nothing.
She is alone.
   Pro.   Then, let her alone.   168
   Val. Not for the world. Why, man, she is mine own,
And I as rich in having such a jewel
As twenty seas, if all their sand were pearl,
The water nectar, and the rocks pure gold.   172
Forgive me that I do not dream on thee,
Because thou see'st me dote upon my love.
My foolish rival, that her father likes
Only for his possessions are so huge,   176
Is gone with her along, and I must after,
For love, thou know'st, is full of jealousy.
   Pro. But she loves you?
   Val. Ay, and we are betroth'd; nay, more, our mar-
       riage-hour,   180
With all the cunning manner of our flight,
Determin'd of: how I must climb her window,

156 except against: *object to*   158 prefer: *advance in station*
168 alone: *peerless*   176: for: *because*

The ladder made of cords, and all the means
Plotted and 'greed on for my happiness.   184
Good Proteus, go with me to my chamber,
In these affairs to aid me with thy counsel.

    Pro. Go on before; I shall inquire you forth.
I must unto the road, to disembark   188
Some necessaries that I needs must use,
And then I'll presently attend you.

    Val. Will you make haste?

    Pro. I will.   *Exit* [*Valentine*]. 192
Even as one heat another heat expels,
Or as one nail by strength drives out another,
So the remembrance of my former love
Is by a newer object quite forgotten.   196
Is it mine [eye], or Valentinus' praise,
Her true perfection, or my false transgression,
That makes me reasonless to reason thus?
She's fair; and so is Julia that I love,—   200
That I did love, for now my love is thaw'd,
Which, like a waxen image 'gainst a fire,
Bears no impression of the thing it was.
Methinks my zeal to Valentine is cold,   204
And that I love him not as I was wont.
O! but I love his lady too-too much;
And that's the reason I love him so little.
How shall I dote on her with more advice,   208
That thus without advice begin to love her?
'Tis but her picture I have yet beheld,
And that hath dazzled my reason's light;
But when I look on her perfections,   212
There is no reason but I shall be blind.

187 forth: *out*
193 Even . . . expels; *cf. n.*
210 picture: *i.e. outer form*

188 road: *anchorage; cf. n. on* I. i. 54
208, 209 advice: *deliberation*
213 no reason but: *no doubt that*

If I can check my erring love, I will;
If not, to compass her I'll use my skill.   [*Exit.*]

Scene Five

[*The Same.   A Street*]

Enter Speed and Launce [severally].

Speed. Launce! by mine honesty, welcome to
Milan!

Launce. Forswear not thyself, sweet youth,
for I am not welcome.   I reckon this always 4
that a man is never undone till he be hanged;
nor never welcome to a place till some certain
shot be paid and the hostess say, 'Welcome!'

Speed. Come on, you madcap, I'll to the 8
alehouse with you presently; where, for one
shot of five pence, thou shalt have five thousand
welcomes.   But, sirrah, how did thy master part
with Madam Julia?   12

Launce. Marry, after they closed in earnest,
they parted very fairly in jest.

Speed. But shall she marry him?

Launce. No.   16

Speed. How then?   Shall he marry her?

Launce. No, neither.

Speed. What, are they broken?

Launce. No, they are both as whole as a fish.   20

Speed. Why then, how stands the matter
with them?

Launce. Marry, thus: when it stands well
with him, it stands well with her.   24

215 compass: *obtain*   7 shot: *tavern-reckoning*
13 closed: *came to terms, or (possibly) embraced*

Speed. What an ass art thou! I understand
thee not.

Launce. What a block art thou, that thou
canst not! My staff understands me.   28

Speed. What thou sayest?

Launce. Ay, and what I do too. Look thee,
I'll but lean, and my staff understands me.

Speed. It stands under thee, indeed.   32

Launce. Why, stand-under and under-stand is all
one.

Speed. But tell me true, will 't be a match?

Launce. Ask my dog. If he say ay, it will; 36
if he say no, it will; if he shake his tail and say
nothing, it will.

Speed. The conclusion is, then, that it will.

Launce. Thou shalt never get such a secret 40
from me but by a parable.

Speed. 'Tis well that I get it so. But, Launce,
how sayest thou, that my master is become a
notable lover?   44

Launce. I never knew him otherwise.

Speed. Than how?

Launce. A notable lubber, as thou reportest
him to be.   48

Speed. Why, thou whoreson ass, thou mis-
takest me.

Launce. Why, fool, I meant not thee; I meant
thy master.   52

Speed. I tell thee, my master is become a hot
lover.

Launce. Why, I tell thee, I care not though
he burn himself in love. If thou wilt, go with 56
me to the alehouse; if not, thou art an

43 how sayest thou: *what have you to say to this*

Hebrew, a Jew, and not worth the name of a
Christian.

   Speed. Why?   60

   Launce. Because thou hast not so much
charity in thee as to go to the ale with a
Christian. Wilt thou go?

   Speed. At thy service.   *Exeunt.* 64

Scene Six

[*The Same.   A Room in the Duke's Palace*]

Enter Proteus solus.

Pro. To leave my Julia, shall I be forsworn;
To love fair Silvia, shall I be forsworn;
To wrong my friend, I shall be much forsworn;
And even that power which gave me first my oath   4
Provokes me to this threefold perjury.
Love bade me swear, and Love bids me forswear.
O sweet-suggesting Love! if thou hast sinn'd,
Teach me, thy tempted subject, to excuse it.   8
At first I did adore a twinkling star,
But now I worship a celestial sun.
Unheedful vows may heedfully be broken;
And he wants wit that wants resolved will   12
To learn his wit to exchange the bad for better.
Fie, fie, unreverend tongue! to call her bad,
Whose sovereignty so oft thou hast preferr'd
With twenty thousand soul-confirming oaths.   16
I cannot leave to love, and yet I do;
But there I leave to love where I should love.
Julia I lose and Valentine I lose.

62, 63 go . . . Christian; *cf. n.*
7 sweet-suggesting: *sweetly seductive*
13 learn: *teach*   17 leave: *cease*

If I keep them, I needs must lose myself;   20
If I lose them, thus find I by their loss,
For Valentine, myself; for Julia, Silvia.
I to myself am dearer than a friend,
For love is still most precious in itself;   24
And Silvia—witness heaven that made her fair!—
Shows Julia but a swarthy Ethiope.
I will forget that Julia is alive,
Remembering that my love to her is dead;   28
And Valentine I'll hold an enemy,
Aiming at Silvia as a sweeter friend.
I cannot now prove constant to myself
Without some treachery us'd to Valentine.   32
This night he meaneth with a corded ladder
To climb celestial Silvia's chamber-window,
Myself in counsel, his competitor.
Now presently, I'll give her father notice   36
Of their disguising and pretended flight;
Who, all enrag'd, will banish Valentine;
For Thurio, he intends, shall wed his daughter;
But, Valentine being gone, I'll quickly cross   40
By some sly trick blunt Thurio's dull proceeding.
Love, lend me wings to make my purpose swift,
As thou hast lent me wit to plot this drift!   *Exit.*

Scene Seven

[*Verona. A Room in Julia's House*]

Enter Julia and Lucetta.

Jul. Counsel, Lucetta; gentle girl, assist me;
And e'en in kind love I do conjure thee,

---

35 competitor: *associate, confidant*   37 pretended: *intended*
41 blunt: *stupid*   43 drift: *scheme*

Who art the table wherein all my thoughts
Are visibly character'd and engrav'd,   4
To lesson me and tell me some good mean
How, with my honour, I may undertake
A journey to my loving Proteus.

   Luc. Alas! the way is wearisome and long.   8

   Jul. A true-devoted pilgrim is not weary
To measure kingdoms with his feeble steps;
Much less shall she that hath Love's wings to fly,
And when the flight is made to one so dear,   12
Of such divine perfection, as Sir Proteus.

   Luc. Better forbear till Proteus make return.

   Jul. O! know'st thou not his looks are my soul's
     food?
Pity the dearth that I have pined in,   16
By longing for that food so long a time.
Didst thou but know the inly touch of love,
Thou wouldst as soon go kindle fire with snow
As seek to quench the fire of love with words.   20

   Luc. I do not seek to quench your love's hot fire,
But qualify the fire's extreme rage,
Lest it should burn above the bounds of reason.

   Jul. The more thou damm'st it up, the more it
     burns.   24
The current that with gentle murmur glides,
Thou know'st, being stopp'd, impatiently doth rage;
But when his fair course is not hindered,
He makes sweet music with th' enamell'd stones,   28
Giving a gentle kiss to every sedge
He overtaketh in his pilgrimage;
And so by many winding nooks he strays
With willing sport, to the wild ocean.   32

3 table: *tablet for memoranda*   4 character'd: *inscribed*
18 inly: *inward*

Then let me go and hinder not my course.
I'll be as patient as a gentle stream
And make a pastime of each weary step,
Till the last step have brought me to my love;   36
And there I'll rest, as after much turmoil
A blessed soul doth in Elysium.

Luc. But in what habit will you go along?

Jul. Not like a woman; for I would prevent   40
The loose encounters of lascivious men.
Gentle Lucetta, fit me with such weeds
As may beseem some well-reputed page.

Luc. Why, then, your ladyship must cut your hair. 44

Jul. No, girl; I'll knit it up in silken strings
With twenty odd-conceited true-love knots.
To be fantastic may become a youth
Of greater time than I shall show to be.   48

Luc. What fashion, madam, shall I make your
      breeches?

Jul. That fits as well as 'Tell me, good my lord,
What compass will you wear your farthingale?'
Why, even what fashion thou best lik'st, Lucetta.   52

Luc. You must needs have them with a cod-piece,
      madam.

Jul. Out, out, Lucetta! that will be ill-favour'd.

Luc. A round hose, madam, now's not worth a pin,
Unless you have a cod-piece to stick pins on.   56

Jul. Lucetta, as thou lov'st me, let me have
What thou think'st meet and is most mannerly.
But tell me, wench, how will the world repute me
For undertaking so unstaid a journey?   60
I fear me, it will make me scandaliz'd.

41 encounters: *accostings*
48 time: *years*
53 cod-piece; *cf. n.*
55 round hose; *cf. n.*
61 scandaliz'd: *disgraced, subject to scandal*

47 fantastic: *fanciful, capricious*
51 farthingale: *hooped petticoat*
54 ill-favour'd: *ill-looking*
60 unstaid: *unbecoming*

Luc. If you think so, then stay at home and go not.

Jul. Nay, that I will not.

Luc. Then never dream on infamy, but go.   64

If Proteus like your journey when you come,

No matter who's displeas'd when you are gone.

I fear me, he will scarce be pleas'd withal.

Jul. That is the least, Lucetta, of my fear.   68

A thousand oaths, an ocean of his tears,

And instances of infinite of love

Warrant me welcome to my Proteus.

Luc. All these are servants to deceitful men.   72

Jul. Base men, that use them to so base effect;

But truer stars did govern Proteus' birth;

His words are bonds, his oaths are oracles,

His love sincere, his thoughts immaculate,   76

His tears pure messengers sent from his heart,

His heart as far from fraud.as heaven from earth.

Luc. Pray heaven he prove so when you come to
him!

Jul. Now, as thou lov'st me, do him not that wrong 80

To bear a hard opinion of his truth.

Only deserve my love by loving him,

And presently go with me to my chamber,

To take a note of what I stand in need of   84

To furnish me upon my longing journey.

All that is mine I leave at thy dispose,

My goods, my lands, my reputation;

Only, in lieu thereof, dispatch me hence.   88

Come, answer not, but to it presently!

I am impatient of my tarriance.   *Exeunt.*

67 withal: *with it*   70 infinite: *infinity*
85 longing: *prompted by longing*   86 dispose: *disposal*
90 tarriance: *delay*

ACT THIRD

Scene One

[Milan.   An anteroom in the Duke's Palace]

Enter Duke, Thurio, [and] Proteus; [and later,] Valentine, Launce, [and] Speed.

Duke. Sir Thurio, give us leave, I pray, awhile;
We have some secrets to confer about.   *[Exit Thurio.]*
Now tell me, Proteus, what's your will with me?
   Pro. My gracious lord, that which I would discover   4
The law of friendship bids me to conceal;
But when I call to mind your gracious favours
Done to me, undeserving as I am,
My duty pricks me on to utter that   8
Which else no worldly good should draw from me.
Know, worthy prince, Sir Valentine, my friend,
This night intends to steal away your daughter.
Myself am one made privy to the plot.   12
I know you have determin'd to bestow her
On Thurio, whom your gentle daughter hates;
And should she thus be stol'n away from you,
It would be much vexation to your age.   16
Thus, for my duty's sake, I rather chose
To cross my friend in his intended drift,
Than, by concealing it, heap on your head
A pack of sorrows which would press you down,   20
Being unprevented, to your timeless grave.
   Duke. Proteus, I thank thee for thine honest care,
Which to requite, command me while I live.
This love of theirs myself have often seen,   24

---

1 give . . . leave: *polite form of dismissal*   4 discover: *disclose*
18 drift: *scheme*   21 timeless: *untimely*

Haply when they have judg'd me fast asleep,
And oftentimes have purpos'd to forbid
Sir Valentine her company and my court;
But fearing lest my jealous aim might err   28
And so unworthily disgrace the man,—
A rashness that I ever yet have shunn'd,—
I gave him gentle looks, thereby to find
That which thyself hast now disclos'd to me.   32
And, that thou mayst perceive my fear of this,
Knowing that tender youth is soon suggested,
I nightly lodge her in an upper tower,
The key whereof myself have ever kept;   36
And thence she cannot be convey'd away.

   Pro. Know, noble lord, they have devis'd a mean
How he her chamber-window will ascend
And with a corded ladder fetch her down;   40
For which the youthful lover now is gone
And this way comes he with it presently;
Where, if it please you, you may intercept him.
But, good my lord, do it so cunningly   44
That my discovery be not aimed at;
For love of you, not hate unto my friend,
Hath made me publisher of this pretence.

   Duke. Upon mine honour, he shall never know   48
That I had any light from thee of this.

   Pro. Adieu, my lord; Sir Valentine is coming.
                                [Exit.]

              [Enter Valentine.]

   Duke. Sir Valentine, whither away so fast?

   Val. Please it your Grace, there is a messenger   52
That stays to bear my letters to my friends,

---

28 aim: *conjecture*   34 suggested: *led astray*
45 discovery: *disclosure*   aimed at: *guessed*
47 pretence: *intention*

And I am going to deliver them.

    Duke. Be they of much import?

    Val. The tenour of them doth but signify   **56**
My health and happy being at your court.

    Duke. Nay then, no matter; stay with me awhile;
I am to break with thee of some affairs
That touch me near, wherein thou must be secret.   **60**
'Tis not unknown to thee that I have sought
To match my friend Sir Thurio to my daughter.

    Val. I know it well, my lord; and sure, the match
Were rich and honourable; besides, the gentleman   **64**
Is full of virtue, bounty, worth, and qualities
Beseeming such a wife as your fair daughter.
Cannot your Grace win her to fancy him?

    Duke. No, trust me; she is peevish, sullen, fro-
        ward,   **68**
Proud, disobedient, stubborn, lacking duty;
Neither regarding that she is my child,
Nor fearing me as if I were her father;
And, may I say to thee, this pride of hers,   **72**
Upon advice, hath drawn my love from her;
And, where I thought the remnant of mine age
Should have been cherish'd by her childlike duty,
I now am full resolv'd to take a wife   **76**
And turn her out to who will take her in.
Then let her beauty be her wedding-dower;
For me and my possessions she esteems not.

    Val. What would your Grace have me to **do in**
        this?   **80**

    Duke. There is a lady of Verona here,
Whom I affect; but she is nice and coy
And nought esteems my aged eloquence.

---

59 break with thee of: *disclose to thee*   67 fancy: *love*
73 advice: *deliberation*   74 where: *whereas*
82 nice: *fastidious*

Now therefore, would I have thee to my tutor,—   84
For long agone I have forgot to court;
Besides, the fashion of the time is chang'd,—
How and which way I may bestow myself
To be regarded in her sun-bright eye.   88

Val. Win her with gifts, if she respect not words.
Dumb jewels often in their silent kind
More than quick words do move a woman's mind.

Duke. But she did scorn a present that I sent her. 92

Val. A woman sometime scorns what best contents
    her.
Send her another; never give her o'er,
For scorn at first makes after-love the more.
If she do frown, 'tis not in hate of you,   96
But rather to beget more love in you;
If she do chide, 'tis not to have you gone;
For why the fools are mad if left alone.
Take no repulse, whatever she doth say;   100
For 'get you gone,' she doth not mean 'away!'
Flatter and praise, commend, extol their graces;
Though ne'er so black, say they have angels' faces.
That man that hath a tongue, I say, is no man,   104
If with his tongue he cannot win a woman.

Duke. But she I mean is promis'd by her friends
Unto a youthful gentleman of worth,
And kept severely from resort of men,   108
That no man hath access by day to her.

Val. Why then, I would resort to her by night.

Duke. Ay, but the doors be lock'd and keys kept
    safe,
That no man hath recourse to her by night.   112

85 forgot: *forgotten how*   87 bestow: *conduct*
89 respect: *heed*   90 kind: *nature*
99 For why: *because*
101 *When she says 'away!' she does not mean 'get you gone!'*
103 black: *dark-complexioned*   109, 112 That: *so that*

Val. What lets but one may enter at her window?

Duke. Her chamber is aloft, far from the ground,
And built so shelving that one cannot climb it
Without apparent hazard of his life.   116

Val. Why then, a ladder quaintly made of cords,
To cast up, with a pair of anchoring hooks,
Would serve to scale another Hero's tower,
So bold Leander would adventure it.   120

Duke. Now, as thou art a gentleman of blood,
Advise me where I may have such a ladder.

Val. When would you use it? Pray, sir, tell me that.

Duke. This very night; for Love is like a child,   124
That longs for everything that he can come by.

Val. By seven o'clock I'll get you such a ladder.

Duke. But hark thee; I will go to her alone.
How shall I best convey the ladder thither?   128

Val. It will be light, my lord, that you may bear it
Under a cloak that is of any length.

Duke. A cloak as long as thine will serve the turn?

Val. Ay, my good lord.

Duke.   Then let me see thy cloak; 132
I'll get me one of such another length.

Val. Why, any cloak will serve the turn, my lord.

Duke. How shall I fashion me to wear a cloak?
I pray thee, let me feel thy cloak upon me.   136

                                 [*Pulls open Valentine's cloak.*]

What letter is this same? What's here?—*To Silvia!*
And here an engine fit for my proceeding!
I'll be so bold to break the seal for once.   [*Reads.*]
'My thoughts do harbour with my Silvia nightly;   140

---

113 lets: *hinders*   116 apparent: *obvious*
117 quaintly: *skilfully*
119, 120 Hero's . . . Leander; *cf. n. on I. i.* 22
120 So: *provided that*   121 blood: *good parentage*
130 of any length: *tolerably long*   131 turn: *occasion*
133 such another: *the same*
138 engine: *contrivance* (*the rope ladder*)   140 harbour: *lodge*

    And slaves they are to me that send them flying.
O! could their master come and go as lightly,
    Himself would lodge where senseless they are lying!
My herald thoughts in thy pure bosom rest them;   144
    While I, their king, that thither them importune,
Do curse the grace that with such grace hath bless'd
    them,
    Because myself do want my servants' fortune.
I curse myself, for they are sent by me,   148
That they should harbour where their lord would be.'
What's here?
       'Silvia, this night I will enfranchise thee.'
'Tis so; and here's the ladder for the purpose.   152
Why, Phaethon,—for thou art Merops' son,—
Wilt thou aspire to guide the heavenly car
And with thy daring folly burn the world?
Wilt thou reach stars, because they shine on thee?   156
Go, base intruder! overweening slave!
Bestow thy fawning smiles on equal mates,
And think my patience, more than thy desert,
Is privilege for thy departure hence.   160
Thank me for this more than for all the favours
Which all too much I have bestow'd on thee.
But if thou linger in my territories
Longer than swiftest expedition   164
Will give thee time to leave our royal court,
By heaven! my wrath shall far exceed the love
I ever bore my daughter or thyself.
Be gone! I will not hear thy vain excuse;   168
But, as thou lov'st thy life, make speed from hence.
                        [Exit.]

142 lightly: *easily*   143 senseless: *insensible*
144 herald: *bearing messages*   145 importune: *command*
146 grace . . . grace; *cf. n.*
153 Phaethon . . . Merops' son; *cf. n.*
160 Is privilege for: *grants the privilege of*

Val. And why not death rather than living torment?
To die is to be banish'd from myself;
And Silvia is myself.   Banish'd from her   172
Is self from self,—a deadly banishment!
What light is light, if Silvia be not seen?
What joy is joy, if Silvia be not by?
Unless it be to think that she is by   176
And feed upon the shadow of perfection.
Except I be by Silvia in the night,
There is no music in the nightingale;
Unless I look on Silvia in the day,   180
There is no day for me to look upon.
She is my essence; and I leave to be,
If I be not by her fair influence
Foster'd, illumin'd, cherish'd, kept alive.   184
I fly not death, to fly his deadly doom.
Tarry I here, I but attend on death;
But, fly I hence, I fly away from life.

[*Enter Proteus and Launce.*]

Pro. Run, boy; run, run, and seek him out.   188
Launce. Soho! soho!
Pro. What seest thou?
Launce. Him we go to find.   There's not a
hair on's head but 'tis a Valentine.   192
Pro. Valentine?
Val. No.
Pro. Who then?   His spirit?
Val. Neither.   196
Pro. What then?
Val. Nothing.

177 shadow: *illusion*   183 influence; *cf. n.*
185 I . . . doom; *cf. n.*   186 attend on: *wait for*
189 Soho; *cf. n.*   192, 193 Valentine.   Valentine? *cf. n.*

Launce. Can nothing speak? Master, shall I
strike?   200
  Pro. Who would'st thou strike?
  Launce. Nothing.
  Pro. Villain, forbear.
Launce. Why, sir, I'll strike nothing.   I pray
you,—   204
  Pro. Sirrah, I say, forbear.—Friend Valentine, a
word.
  Val. My ears are stopp'd and cannot hear good
news,
So much of bad already hath possess'd them.
  Pro. Then in dumb silence will I bury mine,   208
For they are harsh, untuneable and bad.
  Val. Is Silvia dead?
  Pro. No, Valentine.
  Val. No Valentine, indeed, for sacred Silvia!   212
Hath she forsworn me?
  Pro. No, Valentine.
  Val. No Valentine, if Silvia have forsworn me!
What is your news?   216
  Launce. Sir, there is a proclamation that you are
vanished.
  Pro. That thou art banished, O, that's the news,
From hence, from Silvia, and from me thy friend.
  Val. O, I have fed upon this woe already,   220
And now excess of it will make me surfeit.
Doth Silvia know that I am banished?
  Pro. Ay, ay; and she hath offer'd to the doom—
Which, unrevers'd, stands in effectual force—   224
A sea of melting pearl, which some call tears.
Those at her father's churlish feet she tender'd;
With them, upon her knees, her humble self;

Wringing her hands, whose whiteness so became
    them   228
As if but now they waxed pale for woe.
But neither bended knees, pure hands held up,
Sad sighs, deep groans, nor silver-shedding tears,
Could penetrate her uncompassionate sire;   232
But Valentine, if he be ta'en, must die.
Besides, her intercession chaf'd him so,
When she for thy repeal was suppliant,
That to close prison he commanded her,   236
With many bitter threats of biding there.
  Val. No more; unless the next word that thou
    speak'st
Have some malignant power upon my life.
If so, I pray thee, breathe it in mine ear,   240
As ending anthem of my endless dolour.
  Pro. Cease to lament for that thou canst not help,
And study help for that which thou lament'st.
Time is the nurse and breeder of all good.   244
Here if thou stay, thou canst not see thy love;
Besides, thy staying will abridge thy life.
Hope is a lover's staff; walk hence with that
And manage it against despairing thoughts.   248
Thy letters may be here, though thou art hence;
Which, being writ to me, shall be deliver'd
Even in the milk-white bosom of thy love.
The time now serves not to expostulate.   252
Come, I'll convey thee through the city-gate,
And, ere I part with thee, confer at large
Of all that may concern thy love-affairs.
As thou lov'st Silvia, though not for thyself, 256
Regard thy danger, and along with me!

235 repeal: *recall*   241 anthem: *song of grief*
248 manage: *wield*   252 expostulate: *discuss*
256 though: *even though*

Val. I pray thee, Launce, and if thou seest my boy,
Bid him make haste and meet me at the North-gate.

Pro. Go, sirrah, find him out. Come, Valentine. 260

Val. O my dear Silvia! hapless Valentine!

[*Exeunt Valentine and Proteus.*]

Launce. I am but a fool, look you; and yet I
have the wit to think my master is a kind of a
knave; but that's all one, if he be but one knave. 264
He lives not now that knows me to be in love;
yet I am in love; but a team of horse shall
not pluck that from me, nor who 'tis I love; and
yet 'tis a woman; but what woman, I will not 268
tell myself; and yet 'tis a milkmaid; yet 'tis
not a maid, for she hath had gossips; yet 'tis a
maid, for she is her master's maid, and serves
for wages. She hath more qualities than a 272
water-spaniel, — which is much in a bare
Christian. [*Pulling out a paper.*] Here is the
catalog of her condition. 'Imprimis: She
can fetch and carry.' Why, a horse can do no 276
more; nay, a horse cannot fetch, but only carry;
therefore, is she better than a jade. 'Item: She
can milk'; look you, a sweet virtue in a maid
with clean hands.   280

[*Enter Speed.*]

Speed. How now, Signior Launce! what news
with your mastership?

Launce. With my master's ship? why, it is
at sea.   284

264 that's . . . knave; *cf. n.*   266 horse: *horses*
270 gossips: *sponsors for a child of hers*
273 water-spaniel; *cf. n.*   bare: *mere*
275 condition: *characteristics*   Imprimis: *in the first place*
278 jade; *cf. n.*

Speed. Well, your old vice still: mistake the word. What news, then, in your paper?

Launce. The blackest news that ever thou heardest.   288

Speed. Why, man, how black?

Launce. Why, as black as ink.

Speed. Let me read them.

Launce. Fie on thee, jolthead! thou canst 292 not read.

Speed. Thou liest; I can.

Launce. I will try thee. Tell me this: who begot thee?   296

Speed. Marry, the son of my grandfather.

Launce. O, illiterate loiterer! it was the son of thy grandmother. This proves that thou canst not read.   300

Speed. Come, fool, come; try me in thy paper.

Launce. There; and Saint Nicholas be thy speed!   304

Speed. [*Reads.*] 'Imprimis: She can milk.'

Launce. Ay, that she can.

Speed. 'Item: She brews good ale.'

Launce. And thereof comes the proverb, 308 'Blessing of your heart, you brew good ale.'

Speed. 'Item: She can sew.'

Launce. That's as much as to say, 'Can she so?'   312

Speed. 'Item: She can knit.'

Launce. What need a man care for a stock with a wench, when she can knit him a stock?

Speed. 'Item: She can wash and scour.'   316

---

292 jolthead: *blockhead*   298 loiterer: *idler*
303 Saint Nicholas: *patron saint of scholars*
314 stock: *dowry*   315 stock: *stocking*

Launce. A special virtue; for then she need not be washed and scoured.

Speed. 'Item: She can spin.'

Launce. Then may I set the world on wheels, 320 when she can spin for her living.

Speed. 'Item: She hath many nameless virtues.'

Launce. That's as much as to say, bastard 324 virtues; that, indeed, know not their fathers, and therefore have no names.

Speed. Here follow her vices.

Launce. Close at the heels of her virtues.   328

Speed. 'Item: She is not to be [kissed] fasting, in respect of her breath.'

Launce. Well, that fault may be mended with a breakfast. Read on.   332

Speed. 'Item: She hath a sweet mouth.'

Launce. That makes amends for her sour breath.

Speed. 'Item: She doth talk in her sleep.'   336

Launce. It's no matter for that, so she sleep not in her talk.

Speed. 'Item: She is slow in words.'

Launce. O villain, that set this down among 340 her vices! To be slow in words is a woman's only virtue. I pray thee, out with 't, and place it for her chief virtue.

Speed. 'Item: She is proud.'   344

Launce. Out with that too; it was Eve's legacy, and cannot be ta'en from her.

Speed. 'Item: She hath no teeth.'

Launce. I care not for that neither, because 348 I love crusts.

320 set . . . wheels: *live at ease*   322 nameless: *inexpressible*
333 sweet mouth: *sweet tooth*   345 Eve's legacy; *cf. n.*

Speed. 'Item: She is curst.'

Launce. Well, the best is, she hath no teeth
to bite.   352

Speed. 'Item: She will often praise her liquor.'

Launce. If her liquor be good, she shall; if
she will not, I will; for good things should be
praised.   356

Speed. 'Item: She is too liberal.'

Launce. Of her tongue she cannot, for that's
writ down she is slow of; of her purse she shall
not, for that I'll keep shut. Now, of another 360
thing she may, and that cannot I help. Well,
proceed.

Speed. 'Item: She hath more hair than wit,
and more faults than hairs, and more wealth 364
than faults.'

Launce. Stop there; I'll have her. She was
mine, and not mine, twice or thrice in that last
article. Rehearse that once more.   368

Speed. 'Item: She hath more hair than
wit,'—

Launce. More hair than wit it may be;
I'll prove it. The cover of the salt hides the 372
salt, and therefore it is more than the salt; the
hair that covers the wit is more than the wit,
for the greater hides the less. What's next?

Speed. 'And more faults than hairs,'—   376

Launce. That's monstrous! O, that that
were out!

Speed. 'And more wealth than faults.'

Launce. Why, that word makes the faults 380

---

350 curst: *shrewish*   353 praise: *appraise*
357 liberal: *bold, wanton*
363 more . . . wit: *a proverbial expression*

gracious. Well, I'll have her; and if it be a match, as nothing is impossible,—

Speed. What then?

Launce. Why, then will I tell thee,—that thy 384 master stays for thee at the North-gate.

Speed. For me?

Launce. For thee! ay; who art thou? He hath stayed for a better man than thee.   388

Speed. And must I go to him?

Launce. Thou must run to him, for thou hast stayed so long that going will scarce serve the turn.   392

Speed. Why didst not tell me sooner? Pox of your love-letters!   [*Exit.*]

Launce. Now will he be swing'd for reading my letter. An unmannerly slave, that will thrust 396 himself into secrets. I'll after, to rejoice in the boy's correction.   [*Exit.*]

Scene Two

[*The Same.   A Room in the Duke's Palace*]

Enter Duke [and] Thurio; [and later,] Proteus.

Duke. Sir Thurio, fear not but that she will love you,
Now Valentine is banish'd from her sight.

Thu. Since his exile she hath despis'd me most,
Forsworn my company and rail'd at me,   4
That I am desperate of obtaining her.

Duke. This weak impress of love is as a figure
Trenched in ice, which with an hour's heat

381 gracious: *acceptable*   398 correction: *punishment*
5 desperate: *without hope*   7 Trenched: *cut*

Dissolves to water and doth lose his form.   8
A little time will melt her frozen thoughts,
And worthless Valentine shall be forgot.

[*Enter Proteus.*]

How now, Sir Proteus! Is your countryman
According to our proclamation gone?   12
　Pro. Gone, my good lord.
　Duke. My daughter takes his going grievously.
　Pro. A little time, my lord, will kill that grief.
　Duke. So I believe; but Thurio thinks not so.   16
Proteus, the good conceit I hold of thee,—
For thou hast shown some sign of good desert,—
Makes me the better to confer with thee.
　Pro. Longer than I prove loyal to your Grace   20
Let me not live to look upon your Grace.
　Duke. Thou know'st how willingly I would effect
The match between Sir Thurio and my daughter.
　Pro. I do, my lord.   24
　Duke. And also, I think, thou art not ignorant
How she opposes her against my will.
　Pro. She did, my lord, when Valentine was here.
　Duke. Ay, and perversely she persevers so.   28
What might we do to make the girl forget
The love of Valentine, and love Sir Thurio?
　Pro. The best way is to slander Valentine
With falsehood, cowardice, and poor descent,   32
Three things that women highly hold in hate.
　Duke. Ay, but she'll think that it is spoke in hate.
　Pro. Ay, if his enemy deliver it;
Therefore it must with circumstance be spoken   36
By one whom she esteemeth as his friend.
　Duke. Then you must undertake to slander him.

14 grievously: *sorrowfully*　　　　　　17 conceit: *opinion*
36 circumstance: *much detail*

    Pro. And that, my lord, I shall be loath to do:
'Tis an ill office for a gentleman,   40
Especially against his very friend.
    Duke. Where your good word cannot advantage him,
Your slander never can endamage him;
Therefore the office is indifferent,   44
Being entreated to it by your friend.
    Pro. You have prevail'd, my lord. If I can do it,
By aught that I can speak in his dispraise,
She shall not long continue love to him.   48
But say this weed her love from Valentine,
It follows not that she will love Sir Thurio.
    Thu. Therefore, as you unwind her love from him,
Lest it should ravel and be good to none,   52
You must provide to bottom it on me;
Which must be done by praising me as much
As you in worth dispraise Sir Valentine.
    Duke. And, Proteus, we dare trust you in this
      kind,   56
Because we know, on Valentine's report,
You are already Love's firm votary
And cannot soon revolt and change your mind.
Upon this warrant shall you have access   60
Where you with Silvia may confer at large;
For she is lumpish, heavy, melancholy,
And, for your friend's sake, will be glad of you;
Where you may temper her, by your persuasion   64
To hate young Valentine and love my friend.
    Pro. As much as I can do I will effect.
But you, Sir Thurio, are not sharp enough;
You must lay lime to tangle her desires   68

41 very: *true*   44 indifferent: *neither good nor bad*
45 your friend: *i.e. the Duke*   52 ravel: *become entangled*
53 bottom it; *cf. n.*   62 lumpish: *spiritless*
64 temper: *mould*   68 lime: *bird lime*   tangle: *ensnare*

By wailful sonnets, whose composed rimes
Should be full-fraught with serviceable vows.
  Duke. Ay,
Much is the force of heaven-bred poesy.   72
  Pro. Say that upon the altar of her beauty
You sacrifice your tears, your sighs, your heart.
Write till your ink be dry, and with your tears
Moist it again, and frame some feeling line   76
That may discover such integrity;
For Orpheus' lute was strung with poets' sinews,
Whose golden touch could soften steel and stones,
Make tigers tame and huge leviathans   80
Forsake unsounded deeps to dance on sands.
After your dire-lamenting elegies,
Visit by night your lady's chamber-window
With some sweet consort; to their instruments   84
Tune a deploring dump; the night's dead silence
Will well become such sweet-complaining grievance.
This, or else nothing, will inherit her.
  Duke. This discipline shows thou hast been in
      love.   88
  Thu. And thy advice this night I'll put in practice.
Therefore, sweet Proteus, my direction-giver,
Let us into the city presently
To sort some gentlemen well skill'd in music.   92
I have a sonnet that will serve the turn
To give the onset to thy good advice.
  Duke. About it, gentlemen!
  Pro. We'll wait upon your grace till after supper,   96

70 serviceable: *devoted*
77 discover such integrity: *disclose such true devotion*
78 sinews: *nerves*   84 consort: *company of musicians*
85 dump: *mournful melody*   86 grievance: *grieving*
87 inherit: *obtain*   88 discipline: *instruction*
92 sort: *select*
94 give . . . to: *make a beginning of following*

And afterward determine our proceedings.

Duke. Even now about it! I will pardon you.

Exeunt.

ACT FOURTH

Scene One

[*A forest between Milan and Verona*]

Enter Valentine, Speed, and [*at another door*] *certain Outlaws.*

1. Out. Fellows, stand fast; I see a passenger.

2. Out. If there be ten, shrink not, but down with 'em.

3. Out. Stand, sir, and throw us that you have about ye.

If not, we'll make you sit and rifle you.　　　　　　　4

Speed. Sir, we are undone; these are the villains

That all the travellers do fear so much.

Val. My friends,—

1. Out. That's not so, sir; we are your enemies.　　8

2. Out. Peace! we'll hear him.

3. Out. Ay, by my beard, will we, for he is a proper man.

Val. Then know, that I have little wealth to lose.

A man I am cross'd with adversity;　　　　　　　　12

My riches are these poor habiliments,

Of which if you should here disfurnish me,

You take the sum and substance that I have.

2. Out. Whither travel you?　　　　　　　　　16

Val. To Verona.

1. Out. Whence came you?

98 pardon: *excuse*　　　　　　　1 passenger: *passer-by, traveler*
10 proper: *handsome*

Val. From Milan.

3. Out. Have you long sojourn'd there?   20

Val. Some sixteen months; and longer might have
stay'd,

If crooked fortune had not thwarted me.

2. Out. What! were you banish'd thence?

Val. I was.   24

2. Out. For what offence?

Val. For that which now torments me to rehearse.

I kill'd a man, whose death I much repent;

But yet I slew him manfully, in fight,   28

Without false vantage or base treachery.

1. Out. Why, ne'er repent it, if it were done so.

But were you banish'd for so small a fault?

Val. I was, and held me glad of such a doom.   32

2. Out. Have you the tongues?

Val. My youthful travel therein made me happy,

Or else I often had been miserable.

3. Out. By the bare scalp of Robin Hood's fat
friar,   36

This fellow were a king for our wild faction!

1. Out. We'll have him. Sirs, a word.

Speed. Master, be one of them;

It is an honourable kind of thievery.   40

Val. Peace, villain!

2. Out. Tell us this: have you anything to take to?

Val. Nothing but my fortune.

3. Out. Know then, that some of us are gentlemen, 44

Such as the fury of ungovern'd youth

Thrust from the company of awful men.

Myself was from Verona banished

---

32 glad . . . doom: *i.e. glad to get off so cheaply*
33 tongues: *foreign languages*   36 friar: *Friar Tuck*
42 anything to take to: *any means of subsistence*
46 awful: *commanding respect*

For practising to steal away a lady,   48
An heir, and near allied unto the duke.

  2. Out. And I from Mantua, for a gentleman
Who, in my mood, I stabb'd unto the heart.

  1. Out. And I for such like petty crimes as these. 52
But to the purpose; for we cite our faults,
That they may hold excus'd our lawless lives;
And, partly, seeing you are beautified
With goodly shape, and by your own report   56
A linguist, and a man of such perfection   •
As we do in our quality much want—

  2. Out. Indeed, because you are a banish'd man,
Therefore, above the rest, we parley to you.   60
Are you content to be our general?
To make a virtue of necessity
And live, as we do, in this wilderness?

  3. Out. What say'st thou? Wilt thou be of our con-
    sort?   64
Say ay, and be the captain of us all.
We'll do thee homage and be rul'd by thee,
Love thee as our commander and our king.

  1. Out. But if thou scorn our courtesy, thou diest. 68

  2. Out. Thou shalt not live to brag what we have
    offer'd.

  Val. I take your offer and will live with you,
Provided that you do no outrages
On silly women, or poor passengers.   72

  3. Out. No; we detest such vile, base practices.
Come, go with us; we'll bring thee to our crews,
And show thee all the treasure we have got,
Which, with ourselves, all rest at thy dispose. 76

               Exeunt.

48 practising: *plotting*
58 quality: *occupation*
64 consort: *fellowship*

51 mood: *anger*
60 the rest: *any other reason*
72 silly: *helpless*

Scene Two

[Milan. The Court of the Duke's Palace]

Enter Proteus; [and later,] Thurio, Julia, Host, Musician[s], [and] Silvia.

Pro. Already have I been false to Valentine,
And now I must be as unjust to Thurio.
Under the colour of commending him,
I have access my own love to prefer.   4
But Silvia is too fair, too true, too holy,
To be corrupted with my worthless gifts.
When I protest true loyalty to her,
She twits me with my falsehood to my friend; 8
When to her beauty I commend my vows,
She bids me think how I have been forsworn
In breaking faith with Julia whom I lov'd:
And notwithstanding all her sudden quips, 12
The least whereof would quell a lover's hope,
Yet, spaniel-like, the more she spurns my love,
The more it grows, and fawneth on her still.
But here comes Thurio. Now must we to her window, 16
And give some evening music to her ear.

[Enter Thurio, and Musicians.]

Thu. How now, Sir Proteus! are you crept before us?
Pro. Ay, gentle Thurio; for you know that love
Will creep in service where it cannot go. 20
Thu. Ay; but I hope, sir, that you love not here.
Pro. Sir, but I do; or else I would be hence.
Thu. Who? Silvia?

3 colour: *pretence*   9 commend: *deliver*
12 quips: *sharp utterances*   20 go: *walk*

Pro. Ay, Silvia, for your sake.   24
Thu. I thank you for your own. Now, gentlemen,
Let's tune, and to it lustily a while.

[*Enter Host and Julia behind. Julia in boy's clothes.*]

  Host. Now, my young guest, methinks you're
allycholly. I pray you, why is it?   28
  Jul. Marry, mine host, because I cannot be
merry.
  Host. Come, we'll have you merry. I'll bring
you where you shall hear music, and see the 32
gentleman that you asked for.
  Jul. But shall I hear him speak?
  Host. Ay, that you shall.
  Jul. That will be music.   [*Music plays.*] 36
  Host Hark! hark!
  Jul. Is he among these?
  Host. Ay; but peace! let's hear 'em.

Song.

'Who is Silvia? what is she?   40
    That all our swains commend her?
Holy, fair, and wise is she;
    The heaven such grace did lend her,
That she might admired be.   44

'Is she kind as she is fair?
    For beauty lives with kindness:
Love doth to her eyes repair,
    To help him of his blindness;   48
And, being help'd, inhabits there.

28 allycholly: *i.e. melancholy*   49 inhabits: *dwells*

'Then to Silvia let us sing,
    That Silvia is excelling;
She excels each mortal thing   52
    Upon the dull earth dwelling.
To her let us garlands bring.'

Host. How now! are you sadder than you were before? How do you, man? The music likes 56 you not.

Jul. You mistake; the musician likes me not.

Host. Why, my pretty youth?

Jul. He plays false, father.   60

Host. How? Out of tune on the strings?

Jul. Not so; but yet so false that he grieves my very heart-strings.

Host. You have a quick ear.   64

Jul. Ay; I would I were deaf; it makes me have a slow heart.

Host. I perceive you delight not in music.

Jul. Not a whit,—when it jars so.   68

Host. Hark! what fine change is in the music!

Jul. Ay, that change is the spite.

Host. You would have them always play but one thing?   72

Jul. I would always have one play but one thing. But, host, doth this Sir Proteus that we talk on Often resort unto this gentlewoman?

Host. I will tell you what Launce, his man, 76 told me: he lov'd her out of all nick.

Jul. Where is Launce?

Host. Gone to seek his dog; which to-morrow, by his master's command, he must carry for a 80 present to his lady.

Jul. Peace! stand aside; the company parts.

Pro. Sir Thurio, fear not you.   I will so plead
That you shall say my cunning drift excels.   84

Thu. Where meet we?

Pro. At Saint Gregory's well.

Thu. Farewell.   [*Exeunt Thurio and Musicians.*]

[*Enter Silvia above, at her window.*]

Pro. Madam, good even to your ladyship.   88

Sil. I thank you for your music, gentlemen.
Who is that that spake?

Pro. One, lady, if you knew his pure heart's truth,
You would quickly learn to know him by his voice. 92

Sil. Sir Proteus, as I take it.

Pro. Sir Proteus, gentle lady, and your servant.

Sil. What is your will?

Pro.   That I may compass yours.

Sil. You have your wish; my will is even this: 96
That presently you hie you home to bed.
Thou subtle, perjur'd, false, disloyal man!
Think'st thou I am so shallow, so conceitless,
To be seduced by thy flattery,   100
That hast deceiv'd so many with thy vows?
Return, return, and make thy love amends.
For me, by this pale queen of night I swear,
I am so far from granting thy request   104
That I despise thee for thy wrongful suit,
And by and by intend to chide myself
Even for this time I spend in talking to thee.

Pro. I grant, sweet love, that I did love a lady; 108
But she is dead.

Jul. [*Aside.*] 'Twere false, if I should speak it;
For I am sure she is not buried.

84 drift: *scheme*   98 subtle: *crafty*
99 conceitless: *witless*

Sil. Say that she be; yet Valentine thy friend
Survives, to whom, thyself art witness,   112
I am betroth'd; and art thou not asham'd
To wrong him with thy importunacy?

   Pro. I likewise hear that Valentine is dead.

   Sil. And so suppose am I; for in his grave,   116
Assure thyself my love is buried.

   Pro. Sweet lady, let me rake it from the earth.

   Sil. Go to thy lady's grave and call hers thence;
Or, at the least, in hers sepulchre thine.   120

   Jul. [*Aside.*] He heard not that.

   Pro. Madam, if your heart be so obdurate,
Vouchsafe me yet your picture for my love,
The picture that is hanging in your chamber.   124
To that I'll speak, to that I'll sigh and weep;
For since the substance of your perfect self
Is else devoted, I am but a shadow,
And to your shadow will I make true love.   128

   Jul. [*Aside.*] If 'twere a substance, you would, sure,
      deceive it,
And make it but a shadow, as I am.

   Sil. I am very loath to be your idol, sir;
But, since your falsehood shall become you well   132
To worship shadows and adore false shapes,
Send to me in the morning and I'll send it.
And so, good rest.

   Pro.   As wretches have o'er night
That wait for execution in the morn.   136

         [*Exeunt Proteus and Silvia, severally.*]

   Jul. Host, will you go?

   Host. By my halidom, I was fast asleep.

   Jul. Pray you, where lies Sir Proteus?

127 else: *elsewhere*   shadow: *lifeless person*
128 shadow: *portrait*   138 halidom: *anything regarded as sacred*
139 lies: *lodges, sleeps*

Host. Marry, at my house.   Trust me, I think 140
'tis almost day.

Jul. Not so; but it hath been the longest night
That e'er I watch'd, and the most heaviest.   [*Exeunt.*]

Scene Three

[*The Same*]

Enter Eglamour, [and later,] Silvia.

Egl. This is the hour that Madam Silvia
Entreated me to call, and know her mind:
There's some great matter she'd employ me in.
Madam, Madam!

[*Enter Silvia above, at her window.*]

Sil.   Who calls?
Egl.   Your servant, and your friend; 4
One that attends your ladyship's command.

Sil. Sir Eglamour, a thousand times good morrow.

Egl. As many, worthy lady, to yourself.
According to your ladyship's impose,   8
I am thus early come to know what service
It is your pleasure to command me in.

Sil. O Eglamour, thou art a gentleman—
Think not I flatter, for I swear I do not—   12
Valiant, wise, remorseful, well-accomplish'd.
Thou art not ignorant what dear good will
I bear unto the banish'd Valentine,
Nor how my father would enforce me marry   16
Vain Thurio, whom my very soul abhors.
Thyself hast lov'd; and I have heard thee say

143 watch'd: *remained awake through*   8 impose: *command*
13 remorseful: *full of pity*   14 dear: *affectionate*

No grief did ever come so near thy heart
As when thy lady and thy true love died,   20
Upon whose grave thou vow'dst pure chastity.
Sir Eglamour, I would to Valentine,
To Mantua, where I hear he makes abode;
And, for the ways are dangerous to pass,   24
I do desire thy worthy company,
Upon whose faith and honour I repose.
Urge not my father's anger, Eglamour,
But think upon my grief, a lady's grief,   28
And on the justice of my flying hence,
To keep me from a most unholy match,
Which heaven and fortune still rewards with plagues.
I do desire thee, even from a heart   32
As full of sorrows as the sea of sands,
To bear me company and go with me.
If not, to hide what I have said to thee,
That I may venture to depart alone.   36
   Egl. Madam, I pity much your grievances;
Which since I know they virtuously are plac'd,
I give consent to go along with you,
Recking as little what betideth me   40
As much I wish all good befortune you.
When will you go?
   Sil.   This evening coming.
   Egl. Where shall I meet you?
   Sil.   At Friar Patrick's cell,
Where I intend holy confession.   44
   Egl. I will not fail your ladyship.
Good morrow, gentle lady.
   Sil. Good morrow, kind Sir Eglamour.

                              Exeunt [*severally*].

24 for: *because*   37 grievances:.*distresses*
41 befortune: *befall*

Scene Four

[*The Same*]

Enter Launce [*with his dog; and later enter*] *Proteus,*
Julia, [*and*] *Silvia.*

Launce. When a man's servant shall play the
cur with him, look you, it goes hard; one that
I brought up of a puppy; one that I saved from
drowning, when three or four of his blind bro- 4
thers and sisters went to it. I have taught him,
even as one would say precisely, 'Thus I would
teach a dog.' I was sent to deliver him as a
present to Mistress Silvia from my master, and 8
I came no sooner into the dining-chamber but
he steps me to her trencher and steals her
capon's leg. O! 'tis a foul thing when a cur
cannot keep himself in all companies. I would 12
have, as one should say, one that takes upon
him to be a dog indeed, to be, as it were, a dog
at all things. If I had not had more wit than
he, to take a fault upon me that he did, I think 16
verily he had been hanged for 't; sure as I live, he
had suffered for 't. You shall judge. He thrusts
me himself into the company of three or four
gentleman-like dogs under the duke's table. He 20
had not been there—bless the mark,—a pissing-
while, but all the chamber smelt him. 'Out with
the dog!' says one; 'What cur is that?' says
another; 'Whip him out!' says the third; 'Hang 24
him up!' says the duke. I, having been acquainted
with the smell before, knew it was Crab, and

3 of: *from*
10 me; *cf. n.*   trencher: *wooden plate*
14 a dog at: *adept at*

5 to it: *to their deaths*
12 keep: *restrain*
21 bless the mark; *cf. n.*

goes me to the fellow that whips the dogs.
'Friend,' quoth I, 'you mean to whip the dog?' 28
'Ay, marry, do I,' quoth he. 'You do him the
more wrong,' quoth I; ''twas I did the thing you
wot of.' He makes me no more ado, but whips
me out of the chamber. How many masters 32
would do this for his servant? Nay, I'll be
sworn, I have sat in the stocks for puddings he
hath stolen, otherwise he had been executed;
I have stood on the pillory for geese he hath 36
killed, otherwise he had suffered for 't. Thou
thinkest not of this now. Nay, I remember the
trick you served me when I took my leave of
Madam Silvia. Did not I bid thee still mark me 40
and do as I do? When didst thou see me heave
up my leg and make water against a gentlewoman's farthingale? Didst thou ever see me
do such a trick?   44

[*Enter Proteus, and Julia in boy's clothes.*]

Pro. Sebastian is thy name? I like thee well,
And will employ thee in some service presently.
  Jul. In what you please; I will do what I can.
  Pro. I hope thou wilt. [*To Launce.*] How now, you
    whoreson peasant!   48
Where have you been these two days loitering?
  Launce. Marry, sir, I carried Mistress Silvia
the dog you bade me.
  Pro. And what says she to my little jewel?   52
  Launce. Marry, she says, your dog was a cur,
and tells you, currish thanks is good enough for
such a present.
  Pro. But she received my dog?   56

31 wot: *know*   34 puddings: *animals' intestines (sometimes stuffed)*
48 whoreson: *used in coarse playfulness*

Launce. No, indeed, did she not; here have I
brought him back again.

Pro. What! didst thou offer her this from me?

Launce. Ay, sir; the other squirrel was stolen 60
from me by the hangman boys in the market-
place; and then I offered her mine own, who is
a dog as big as ten of yours, and therefore the
gift the greater. 64

Pro. Go, get thee hence, and find my dog again,
Or ne'er return again into my sight.
Away, I say! Stay'st thou to vex me here?

                          [Exit Launce.]

A slave that still an end turns me to shame. 68
Sebastian, I have entertained thee,
Partly that I have need of such a youth,
That can with some discretion do my business,
For 't is no trusting to yond foolish lout; 72
But chiefly for thy face and thy behaviour,
Which, if my augury deceive me not,
Witness good bringing up, fortune, and truth.
Therefore, know thou, for this I entertain thee. 76
Go presently, and take this ring with thee;
Deliver it to Madam Silvia.
She lov'd me well deliver'd it to me.

Jul. It seems you lov'd not her, to leave her token. 80
She's dead, belike?

Pro.   Not so; I think she lives.

Jul. Alas!

Pro. Why dost thou cry 'alas'?

Jul.   I cannot choose
But pity her. 84

Pro. Wherefore should'st thou pity her?

60 squirrel; *cf. n.*   61 hangman: *fit for the hangman*
68 still an end: *continually*   76 entertain: *take into service*
79 deliver'd: *who delivered*   80 leave: *part with*

Jul. Because methinks that she lov'd you as well
As you do love your lady Silvia.
She dreams on him that has forgot her love;   88
You dote on her that cares not for your love.
'Tis pity love should be so contrary;
And thinking on it makes me cry, 'alas'!

Pro. Well, give her that ring and therewithal   92
This letter. That's her chamber. Tell my lady
I claim the promise for her heavenly picture.
Your message done, hie home unto my chamber,
Where thou shalt find me sad and solitary.   [*Exit.*]

Jul. How many women would do such a message? 97
Alas, poor Proteus! thou hast entertain'd
A fox to be the shepherd of thy lambs.
Alas, poor fool! why do I pity him   100
That with his very heart despiseth me?
Because he loves her, he despiseth me;
Because I love him, I must pity him.
This ring I gave him when he parted from me,   104
To bind him to remember my good will;
And now am I—unhappy messenger—
To plead for that which I would not obtain,
To carry that which I would have refus'd,   108
To praise his faith which I would have disprais'd.
I am my master's true-confirmed love,
But cannot be true servant to my master,
Unless I prove false traitor to myself.   112
Yet will I woo for him; but yet so coldly
As heaven it knows, I would not have him speed.

[*Enter Silvia, attended.*]

Gentlewoman, good day! I pray you, be my mean
To bring me where to speak with Madam Silvia.   116

100 poor fool: *referring to herself*   114 speed: *be successful*

Sil. What would you with her, if that I be she?

Jul. If you be she, I do entreat your patience
To hear me speak the message I am sent on.

Sil. From whom?   120

Jul. From my master, Sir Proteus, madam.

Sil. O! he sends you for a picture?

Jul. Ay, madam.

Sil. Ursula, bring my picture there.   124

                       [A picture brought.]

Go, give your master this.   Tell him from me,
One Julia, that his changing thoughts forget,
Would better fit his chamber than this shadow.

Jul. Madam, please you peruse this letter.—   128
Pardon me, madam, I have unadvis'd
Deliver'd you a paper that I should not.
This is the letter to your ladyship.

Sil. I pray thee, let me look on that again.   132

Jul. It may not be; good madam, pardon me.

Sil. There, hold.
I will not look upon your master's lines.
I know they are stuff'd with protestations   136
And full of new-found oaths, which he will break
As easily as I do tear his paper.

Jul. Madam, he sends your ladyship this ring.

Sil. The more shame for him that he sends it me; 140
For I have heard him say a thousand times,
His Julia gave it him at his departure.
Though his false finger have profan'd the ring,
Mine shall not do his Julia so much wrong.   144

Jul. She thanks you.

Sil. What say'st thou?

Jul. I thank you, madam, that you tender her.
Poor gentlewoman! my master wrongs her much.   148

129 unadvis'd: *inadvertently*   147 tender: *regard tenderly*

Sil. Dost thou know her?

Jul. Almost as well as I do know myself:
To think upon her woes, I do protest
That I have wept a hundred several times.   152

Sil. Belike she thinks that Proteus hath forsook her.

Jul. I think she doth, and that's her cause of sorrow.

Sil. Is she not passing fair?

Jul. She hath been fairer, madam, than she is.   156
When she did think my master lov'd her well,
She, in my judgment, was as fair as you;
But since she did neglect her looking-glass
And threw her sun-expelling mask away,   160
The air hath starv'd the roses in her cheeks
And pinch'd the lily-tincture of her face,
That now she is become as black as I.

Sil. How tall was she?   164

Jul. About my stature; for, at Pentecost,
When all our pageants of delight were play'd,
Our youth got me to play the woman's part,
And I was trimm'd in Madam Julia's gown,   168
Which served me as fit, by all men's judgments,
As if the garment had been made for me.
Therefore I know she is about my height.
And at that time I made her weep agood,   172
For I did play a lamentable part.
Madam, 'twas Ariadne passioning
For Theseus' perjury and unjust flight;
Which I so lively acted with my tears   176
That my poor mistress, moved therewithal,
Wept bitterly, and would I might be dead
If I in thought felt not her very sorrow!

Sil. She is beholding to thee, gentle youth.—   180

165 Pentecost: *Whitsuntide*
166 pageants of delight: *delightful theatrical representations*
168 trimm'd: *dressed*   172 agood: *in earnest*
174 passioning: *sorrowing*   180 beholding: *indebted*

Alas, poor lady, desolate and left!
I weep myself to think upon thy words.
Here, youth, there is my purse. I give thee this
For thy sweet mistress' sake, because thou lov'st
      her.   184
Farewell.
    Jul. And she shall thank you for 't, if e'er you know
    her.—   [*Exit Silvia, with Attendants.*]
A virtuous gentlewoman, mild and beautiful.
I hope my master's suit will be but cold,   188
Since she respects my mistress' love so much.
Alas, how love can trifle with itself!
Here is her picture; let me see; I think,
If I had such a tire, this face of mine   192
Were full as lovely as is this of hers;
And yet the painter flatter'd her a little,
Unless I flatter with myself too much.
Her hair is auburn, mine is perfect yellow: 196
If that be all the difference in his love,
I'll get me such a colour'd periwig.
Her eyes are grey as glass, and so are mine.
Ay, but her forehead's low, and mine's as high.   200
What should it be that he respects in her
But I can make respective in myself,
If this fond Love were not a blinded god?
Come, shadow, come, and take this shadow up,   204
For 'tis thy rival. O thou senseless form!
Thou shalt be worshipp'd, kiss'd, lov'd, and ador'd,
And, were there sense in his idolatry,
My substance should be statue in thy stead.   208
I'll use thee kindly for thy mistress' sake,

188 cold: *ineffectual*
189 my mistress': *repeating the fiction of l. 177*
192 tire: *headdress*   202 respective: *worthy of respect*
204 shadow . . . shadow; *cf. n. on IV. ii. 127, 128*   take . . . up:
    pun on sense of 'oppose'

That us'd me so; or else, by Jove I vow,
I should have scratch'd out your unseeing eyes,
To make my master out of love with thee.   [*Exit.*]

ACT FIFTH

Scene One

[*Milan.   An Abbey*]

Enter Eglamour, [and later,] Silvia.

Egl. The sun begins to gild the western sky,
And now it is about the very hour
That Silvia at Friar Patrick's cell should meet me.
She will not fail; for lovers break not hours,   4
Unless it be to come before their time,
So much they spur their expedition.
See, where she comes.

[*Enter Silvia.*]

                    Lady, a happy evening!
Sil. Amen, amen! go on, good Eglamour,   8
Out at the postern by the abbey-wall.
I fear I am attended by some spies.
Egl. Fear not; the forest is not three leagues off;
If we recover that, we're sure enough.   *Exeunt.*

Scene Two

[*The Same.   A Room in the Duke's Palace*]

Enter Thurio, Proteus, Julia; [and later,] Duke.

Thu. Sir Proteus, what says Silvia to my suit?
Pro. O, sir, I find her milder than she was;

9 postern: *small back or side door*   12 recover: *reach*   sure: *safe*

And yet she takes exceptions at your person.

    Thu. What! that my leg is too long?   4

    Pro. No, that it is too little.

    Thu. I'll wear a boot to make it somewhat rounder.

    [*Jul. Aside.*] But love will not be spurr'd to what it
      loathes.

    Thu. What says she to my face?   8

    Pro. She says it is a fair one.

    Thu. Nay then, the wanton lies; my face is black.

    Pro. But pearls are fair, and the old saying is,

'Black men are pearls in beauteous ladies' eyes.'   12

    [*Jul. Aside.*] 'Tis true, such pearls as put out ladies'
      eyes;

For I had rather wink than look on them.

    Thu. How likes she my discourse?

    Pro. Ill, when you talk of war.   16

    Thu. But well, when I discourse of love and peace?

    Jul. [*Aside.*] But better, indeed, when you hold
      your peace.

    Thu. What says she to my valour?

    Pro. O, sir, she makes no doubt of that.   20

    Jul. [*Aside.*] She needs not, when she knows it
      cowardice.

    Thu. What says she to my birth?

    Pro. That you are well deriv'd.

    Jul. [*Aside.*] True; from a gentleman to a fool.   24

    Thu. Considers she my possessions?

    Pro. O, ay; and pities them.

    Thu. Wherefore?

    Jul. [*Aside.*] That such an ass should owe them.   28

---

3 takes exceptions at: *objects to*
13 pearls: *cataracts*
23 deriv'd: *descended; hence the quibble following*
25, 26 possessions . . . pities; *cf. n.*

9 fair; *cf. n.*

28 owe: *own*

Pro. That they are out by lease.

Jul. Here comes the duke.

[*Enter Duke.*]

Duke. How now, Sir Proteus! how now, Thurio!
Which of you saw Sir Eglamour of late?   32

Thu. Not I.

Pro.   Nor I.

Duke.   Saw you my daughter?

Pro.   Neither.

Duke. Why then,
She's fled unto that peasant Valentine,
And Eglamour is in her company.   36
'Tis true; for Friar Laurence met them both,
As he in penance wander'd through the forest.
Him he knew well, and guess'd that it was she,
But, being mask'd, he was not sure of it.   40
Besides, she did intend confession
At Patrick's cell this even, and there she was not.
These likelihoods confirm her flight from hence.
Therefore, I pray you, stand not to discourse,   44
But mount you presently and meet with me
Upon the rising of the mountain-foot,
That leads towards Mantua, whither they are fled.
Dispatch, sweet gentlemen, and follow me.   [*Exit.*] 48

Thu. Why, this it is to be a peevish girl,
That flies her fortune when it follows her.
I'll after, more to be reveng'd on Eglamour
Than for the love of reckless Silvia.   [*Exit.*] 52

Pro. And I will follow, more for Silvia's love
Than hate of Eglamour that goes with her.   [*Exit.*]

Jul. And I will follow, more to cross that love
Than hate for Silvia that is gone for love. [*Exit.*] 56

29 out by lease: *let out to others*   35 peasant: *base person*
46 mountain-foot: *foothill*   49 peevish: *perverse*

Scene Three

[Frontiers of Mantua.   The Forest]

[Enter] Silvia *[and]* Outlaws.

1. Out. Come, come,
Be patient; we must bring you to our captain.

Sil. A thousand more mischances than this one
Have learn'd me how to brook this patiently.   4

2. Out. Come, bring her away.

1. Out. Where is the gentleman that was with her?

3. Out. Being nimble-footed, he hath outrun us;
But Moyses and Valerius follow him.   8
Go thou with her to the west end of the wood;
There is our captain.   We'll follow him that's fled.
The thicket is beset; he cannot 'scape.

[Exeunt all except the First Outlaw and Silvia.]

1. Out. Come, I must bring you to our captain's
  cave.   12
Fear not; he bears an honourable mind,
And will not use a woman lawlessly.

Sil. O Valentine! this I endure for thee.   *Exeunt.*

Scene Four

[Another Part of the Forest]

Enter Valentine; *[and later,]* Proteus, Silvia, Julia,
    Duke, Thurio, *[and]* Outlaws.

Val. How use doth breed a habit in a man!
This shadowy desert, unfrequented woods,
I better brook than flourishing peopled towns.
Here can I sit alone, unseen of any,   4

4 learn'd: *taught*   brook: *endure*
2 desert: *any uninhabited region*

And to the nightingale's complaining notes
Tune my distresses and record my woes.
O thou that dost inhabit in my breast,
Leave not the mansion so long tenantless,   8
Lest, growing ruinous, the building fall
And leave no memory of what it was!
Repair me with thy presence, Silvia!
Thou gentle nymph, cherish thy forlorn swain!   12
                                        [*Noise within.*]

What halloing and what stir is this to-day?
These are my mates, that make their wills their law,
Have some unhappy passenger in chase.
They love me well; yet I have much to do   16
To keep them from uncivil outrages.
Withdraw thee, Valentine: who's this comes here?
                                        [*Steps aside.*]

[*Enter Proteus, Silvia, and Julia.*]

  Pro. Madam, this service I have done for you—
Though you respect not aught your servant doth—   20
To hazard life and rescue you from him
That would have forc'd your honour and your love.
Vouchsafe me, for my meed, but one fair look;
A smaller boon than this I cannot beg,   24
And less than this, I am sure, you cannot give.
  Val. [*Aside.*] How like a dream is this I see and
    hear!
Love, lend me patience to forbear awhile.
  Sil. O, miserable, unhappy that I am!   28
  Pro. Unhappy were you, madam, ere I came;
But by my coming I have made you happy.
  Sil. By thy approach thou mak'st me most unhappy.

6 record: *sing*   7 inhabit: *lodge*
12 swain: *lover*   15 Have: *who have*
20 respect: *heed*   31 approach: *amatory advance (probably)*

Jul. [*Aside.*] And me, when he approacheth to your
    presence.   32
Sil. Had I been seized by a hungry lion,
I would have been a breakfast to the beast,
Rather than have false Proteus rescue me.
O! heaven be judge how I love Valentine,   36
Whose life's as tender to me as my soul;
And full as much—for more there cannot be—
I do detest false perjur'd Proteus.
Therefore be gone, solicit me no more.   40
    Pro. What dangerous action, stood it next to death,
Would I not undergo for one calm look!
O, 'tis the curse in love, and still approv'd,
When women cannot love where they're belov'd!   44
    Sil. When Proteus cannot love where he's belov'd.
Read over Julia's heart, thy first best love,
For whose dear sake thou didst then rend thy faith
Into a thousand oaths; and all those oaths   48
Descended into perjury to love me.
Thou hast no faith left now, unless thou'dst two,
And that's far worse than none.   Better have none
Than plural faith, which is too much by one.   52
Thou counterfeit to thy true friend!
    Pro.   In love
Who respects friend?
    Sil.   All men but Proteus.
    Pro. Nay, if the gentle spirit of moving words
Can no way change you to a milder form,   56
I'll woo you like a soldier, at arms' end,
And love you 'gainst the nature of love,—force ye.
    Sil. O heaven!
    Pro.   I'll force thee yield to my desire.

37 tender: *precious*   42 calm: *i.e. gentle*
43 still approv'd: *continually confirmed by experience*
54 respects: *takes into account*   57 arms' end: *sword's point*

Val. [*Coming forward.*] Ruffian, let go that rude
   uncivil touch;   60
Thou friend of an ill fashion!
   Pro.   Valentine!
   Val. Thou common friend, that's without faith or
   love—
For such is a friend now! Treacherous man,
Thou hast beguil'd my hopes! Naught but mine eye   64
Could have persuaded me. Now I dare not say
I have one friend alive; thou wouldst disprove me.
Who should be trusted now, when one's right hand
Is perjur'd to the bosom? Proteus,   68
I am sorry I must never trust thee more,
But count the world a stranger for thy sake.
The private wound is deep'st. O time most curst!
'Mongst all foes that a friend should be the worst!   72
   Pro. My shame and guilt confounds me.
Forgive me, Valentine. If hearty sorrow
Be a sufficient ransom for offence,
I tender 't here; I do as truly suffer   76
As e'er I did commit.
   Val.   Then I am paid;
And once again I do receive thee honest.
Who by repentance is not satisfied
Is nor of heaven nor earth; for these are pleas'd.   80
By penitence the Eternal's wrath's appeas'd;
And, that my love may appear plain and free,
All that was mine in Silvia I give thee.
   Jul. O me unhappy!   [*Swoons.*]   84
   Pro. Look to the boy.
   Val. Why, boy! why, wag! how now! what's the
   matter?
Look up; speak.

62 common: *base*   77 commit: *transgress*
78 receive: *acknowledge*

Jul. O good sir, my master charg'd me   88
To deliver a ring to Madam Silvia,
Which out of my neglect was never done.
 Pro. Where is that ring, boy?
 Jul.   Here 'tis; this is it. [*Gives a ring.*]
 Pro. How! let me see.   92
Why this is the ring I gave to Julia.
 Jul. O, cry you mercy, sir; I have mistook;
This is the ring you sent to Silvia.
        [*Shows another ring.*]
 Pro. But how cam'st thou by this ring?   96
At my depart I gave this unto Julia.
 Jul. And Julia herself did give it me;
And Julia herself hath brought it hither.
 Pro. How! Julia!   100
 Jul. Behold her that gave aim to all thy oaths,
And entertain'd them deeply in her heart.
How oft hast thou with perjury cleft the root!
O Proteus! let this habit make thee blush.   104
Be thou asham'd that I have took upon me
Such an immodest raiment, if shame live
In a disguise of love.
It is the lesser blot, modesty finds,   108
Women to change their shapes than men their minds.
 Pro. Than men their minds! 'tis true. O heaven!
  were man
But constant, he were perfect. That one error
Fills him with faults; makes him run through all the
  sins: 112
Inconstancy falls off ere it begins.
What is in Silvia's face, but I may spy
More fresh in Julia's with a constant eye?

94 cry you mercy: *I beg your pardon*
101 gave aim to: *was the object of*
104 habit: *garb*
113 Inconstancy . . . begins; *cf. n.*
103 root: *bottom of the heart*
106, 107 if . . . love; *cf. n.*

Val. Come, come, a hand from either.   116
Let me be blest to make this happy close;
'Twere pity two such friends should be long foes.

Pro. Bear witness, heaven, I have my wish for ever.
Jul. And I mine.   120

[*Enter Outlaws with Duke and Thurio.*]

Out. A prize! a prize! a prize!
Val. Forbear, forbear, I say; it is my lord the duke.
Your Grace is welcome to a man disgrac'd,
Banished Valentine.

Duke.   Sir Valentine!   124
Thu. Yonder is Silvia; and Silvia's mine.
Val. Thurio, give back, or else embrace thy death;
Come not within the measure of my wrath;
Do not name Silvia thine; if once again,   128
Verona shall not hold thee.   Here she stands;
Take but possession of her with a touch,—
I dare thee but to breathe upon my love.

Thu. Sir Valentine, I care not for her, I.   132
I hold him but a fool that will endanger
His body for a girl that loves him not.
I claim her not, and therefore she is thine.

Duke. The more degenerate and base art thou,   136
To make such means for her as thou hast done,
And leave her on such slight conditions.
Now, by the honour of my ancestry,
I do applaud thy spirit, Valentine,   140
And think thee worthy of an empress' love.
Know then, I here forget all former griefs,
Cancel all grudge, repeal thee home again,
Plead a new state in thy unrivall'd merit,   144

117 close: *union*   126 give back: *fall back*   127 measure: *reach*
137 means: *efforts*   138 on . . . conditions: *so easily*
143 repeal: *recall from exile*   144 Plead . . . merit; *cf. n.*

To which I thus subscribe: Sir Valentine,
Thou art a gentleman and well deriv'd;
Take thou thy Silvia, for thou hast deserv'd her.

   Val. I thank your Grace; the gift hath made me
     happy.   148
I now beseech you, for your daughter's sake,
To grant one boon that I shall ask of you.

   Duke. I grant it, for thine own, whate'er it be.

   Val. These banish'd men, that I have kept withal 152
Are men endu'd with worthy qualities:
Forgive them what they have committed here,
And let them be recall'd from their exile.
They are reformed, civil, full of good,   156
And fit for great employment, worthy lord.

   Duke. Thou hast prevail'd; I pardon them, and
     thee;
Dispose of them as thou know'st their deserts.
Come, let us go; we will include all jars   160
With triumphs, mirth, and rare solemnity.

   Val. And as we walk along, I dare be bold
With our discourse to make your Grace to smile.
What think you of this page, my lord?   164

   Duke. I think the boy hath grace in him; he blushes.

   Val. I warrant you, my lord, more grace than boy.

   Duke. What mean you by that saying?

   Val. Please you, I'll tell you as we pass along, 168
That you will wonder what hath fortuned.
Come, Proteus; 'tis your penance but to hear
The story of your loves discovered;
That done, our day of marriage shall be yours; 172
One feast, one house, one mutual happiness. *Exeunt.*

152 kept withal: *lived with*   160 include: *conclude*   jars: *discords*
161 triumphs: *public festivities*   solemnity: *festivity*
169 fortuned: *happened*

FINIS.

NOTES

Dramatis Personæ. In the First Folio the *Dramatis Personæ* ('The names of all the Actors') appear at the end of the play.

I. i. 22. *Leander.* A youth who nightly swam across the Hellespont to visit his beloved Hero. One night he was drowned in his attempt; whereupon Hero also leaped to her death in the Hellespont. Cf. III. i. 119, 120.

I. i. 54. *shipp'd.* Although it may be shown that in Shakespeare's time there was probably some sort of water-route between Verona and Milan, we may assume that the dramatist is merely casual here, having vaguely in mind a departure by sea from London rather than pretending to accuracy in Italian geography and topography.

I. i. 72, 73. *shipp'd . . . sheep.* It appears that in pronunciation these two words were sufficiently similar to allow a pun. Cf. note on I. i. 54.

I. i. 102. *laced mutton.* Apparently a play upon the words 'lost' and 'laced' in this speech is intended. Presumably the similarity between the two words in pronunciation was greater than now.

I. i. 131. *Marry.* A mild interjection, originally the name of the Virgin Mary used as an oath or invocation.

I. i. 160. *destin'd to a drier death on shore.* A reference to the proverbial notion, 'He that is born to be hanged shall never be drowned.'

I. ii. 9. *Sir Eglamour.* This personage is not to be confused with Silvia's friend, who appears later.

I. ii. 66. *stomach.* A play upon the two meanings, 'anger' and 'appetite.'

I. ii. 66, 67. *meat . . . maid.* Probably a quibble, 'meat' being pronounced like 'mate.'

I. ii. 78. *set.* 'Set to music.' The next line quibblingly implies the meaning, 'set store by.'

I. ii. 82. *burden.* Refrain, or, more exactly, a musical figure repeated, throughout the song, in the bass (French *bourdon*) or underpart.

I. ii. 90. *flat.* A quibble on the word in its musical meaning and in the sense of 'downright.'

I. ii. 91, 92. *And mar the concord with too harsh a descant. There wanteth but a mean to fill your song.* 'Descant' means the air sung extempore upon a given bass. The 'mean' is the intermediate part (alto or tenor) between the treble and bass. Here the word 'mean' seems to refer also to the correct pitch of any musical note, precisely between 'sharp' and 'flat' of lines 88 and 90.

I. ii. 94. *bid the base.* A phrase from the game of prisoner's base. Possibly Lucetta 'bids the base' by challenging Julia to pursue her, thus setting free Proteus, the prisoner at the base.

I. ii. 101. *would I were so anger'd with the same.* 'Would that the same letter still existed, and inspired no more anger than I now feel.'

I. iii. 27. *emperor.* We need not infer that Shakespeare had in mind the occasional sojourns of Charles V (Emperor, 1519-1556) at Milan. 'Emperor' here probably refers only to the Duke of Milan.

I. iii. 44. *in good time.* The phrase is equivalent to '*à propos,*' and is often used when a character arrives opportunely.

II. i. 1, 2. *on . . . one.* In the sixteenth century these two words were often spelled alike, and in pronunciation were sufficiently similar to allow a pun.

II. i. 28. *Hallowmas.* All Saints' Day, November 1. On this day beggars often received special alms, including 'soul-cake.'

II. i. 30. *one of the lions.* Possibly a reference to

lions in the Tower of London, or to lions on a royal standard displayed in the theater, or to lions in general.

II. i. 104, 105. *motion . . . puppet . . . interpret.* In a puppet-play, or 'motion,' the manipulator of the puppets supplied a discourse designed to 'interpret' the action.

II. i. 110. *servant.* A man who pays authorized attentions to a lady, without her pledging herself by accepting them.

II. i. 165, 166. *earnest . . . none.* A pun upon 'earnest' as an adjective, and as a noun meaning 'money paid as an instalment to secure a bargain.'

II. i. 177. *speak in print.* The source of the four lines that Speed found 'in print' is not known. They are evidently composed in 'King Cambyses' vein.'

II. iii. 31. *wood.* Possibly there is a pun upon the noun, as indicating a shoe made of wood.

II. iv. 18. *quote.* A quibble is probably intended upon 'quote' in the next line, pronounced to sound like 'coat.'

II. iv. 20. *jerkin, doublet.* The doublet was a loose upper garment; the jerkin, a long jacket worn over the doublet, or in place of it.

II. iv. 28. *live in your air.* The chameleon was supposed to live on air. See II. i. 181.

II. iv. 90. *lock'd in her crystal looks.* This expression probably arises from a belief that a spirit might be inclosed in a crystal sphere and made to obey commands.

II. iv. 153. *principality.* A member of the seventh order of celestial beings. The hierarchy of these beings may be arranged as follows: (1) Seraphim, (2) Cherubim, (3) Thrones, (4) Dominions, (5) Virtues, (6) Powers, (7) Principalities, (8) Archangels, and (9) Angels.

II. iv. 193. *Even as one heat another heat expels.*

Apparently a reference to an old practice of exposing a burned part of the body to a fire, in the belief that external heat expelled the heat from the burn. Cf. *Romeo and Juliet*, I. ii. 46: 'Tut! man, one fire burns out another's burning.'

II. v. 62, 63. *go to the ale with a Christian.* A reference to 'Church-ale,' a village festival at which ale was sold to raise funds for a church.

II. vii. 53. *cod-piece.* A part of a man's breeches made indelicately conspicuous in Shakespeare's time.

II. vii. 55. *round hose.* An article of clothing which covered both legs and loins, and which puffed out at the hips.

III. i. 146. *Do curse the grace that with such grace hath bless'd them. grace . . . grace:* 'graciousness . . . favour.' The first 'grace' may mean either 'gracious person' or 'one of the Graces.'

III. i. 153. *Phaethon . . . Merops' son.* Phaethon's father was Phoebus, and his mother was Clymene, wife of Merops. Phaethon rashly persuaded his father to allow him to drive the chariot of the sun for one day. Failing to control the horses, he came too near the earth, a result referred to in lines 154 and 155. In the classical reference the Duke presumably means merely to taunt Valentine with rashness. It has been suggested, however, that the name Merops provides a pun on the 'ropes' of the ladder.

III. i. 183. *influence.* Probably refers to the 'influence' of a star, in the astrological sense of blessing or protection.

III. i. 185. *I fly not death, to fly his deadly doom.* 'I do not escape death by flying from the Duke's sentence of death.'

III. i. 189. *Soho.* A hunting cry used when a hare is seen. Hence the pun upon 'hair' in Launce's next speech.

III. i. 192, 193. *Valentine. Valentine?* The pun is upon 'valentine' as a token of true-love and 'Valentine' as a proper name. The same pun occurs in lines 212, 215.

III. i. 264. *that's all one, if he be but one knave.* 'That's no matter, if he be but slightly a knave.' 'But one knave' implies degrees in knavery, 'two knaves' being a term for excessive knavery.

III. i. 273. *water-spaniel.* This animal was thought to be especially given to fawning.

III. i. 278. *jade.* Probably a pun upon the meanings 'an ill-conditioned horse' and 'a woman of low morals.'

III. i. 345. *Eve's legacy.* Apparently Launce takes 'proud' of the preceding speech as meaning 'hot-blooded' or 'lascivious.' Possibly there is also an allusion to pride as the original deadly sin.

III. ii. 53. *bottom it.* 'Wind it as a skein or ball of thread on a core, or bottom, of thread or harder material.'

IV. iv. 10. *me.* This equivalent of the Latin 'ethical dative' is used merely to show a certain interest felt by the person indicated. The same use is seen in lines 19 and 27.

IV. iv. 21. *bless the mark.* In its origin probably a formula to avert an evil omen; and hence used also as an apology when something improper or obnoxious is being said.

IV. iv. 60. *squirrel.* Possibly an expression commonly applied to a small dog; or possibly a contemptuous epithet suggested by the fact that sometimes squirrels were actually carried about by ladies.

V. ii. 9. *fair.* The meaning may be 'pale,' with a suggestion of effeminacy; or 'fair-faced,' in the sense of 'deceptive.'

V. ii. 25, 26. *possessions . . . pities.* Probably a quibble upon 'possessions' in the sense of 'property' and 'possessions by spirits.' Hence there is probably a double meaning in 'pities': 'despises' (the property) and 'pities' (the possessions by spirits).

V. iv. 106, 107. *if shame live In a disguise of love.* 'If there be any shame in a disguise assumed because of love'; or, possibly, referring to Proteus' duplicity, 'if there be any shame in one who falsely pretends to love.'

V. iv. 113. *Inconstancy falls off ere it begins.* Probably this means, 'An inconstant man begins to be faithless even before he has declared his love.'

V. iv. 144. *Plead a new state in thy unrivall'd merit.* The meaning of this line is uncertain. The following possibilities are offered: (1) 'Plead (in excuse for my change) that your exhibition of such merit creates a new situation'; (2) 'Plead for a new standing for myself in thy unrivall'd merit'; (3) 'Argue for (or utter) a new estimate of thy unrivall'd merit.'

APPENDIX A

SOURCES OF THE PLAY

Although a considerable number of literary origins have been proposed for one part or another of *The Two Gentlemen of Verona,* the source of the main action is represented best, so far as we now know, by the story of Felix and Felismena in *Diana Enamorada,* a pastoral romance of adventurous incidents written in Spanish by Jorge de Montemayor, and first printed in 1542. This story, we may assume, was accessible to Shakespeare in other forms than the Spanish. Bartholomew Yonge's English translation of *Diana* was not published until 1598; but he tells us that it had been in manuscript for sixteen years, and we know that before 1598 two other English translations of parts of Montemayor's work existed in unpublished form. A French translation of relevant parts of *Diana* was printed in 1578 and 1587. It is possible also that the lost play *Felix and Philiomena,* acted at Greenwich in 1584, treated the same fiction.

Directly or indirectly, then, the main plot of Shakespeare's play seems to derive from Montemayor's story; and although we cannot be sure as to contributions from intermediate sources, a comparison of the play and the Spanish romance probably discloses fairly enough at least the general nature of Shakespeare's indebtedness to predecessors, and the direction of his originality. Among the chief matters in which the play resembles the narrative are the following: Proteus' employing Julia's maid as intermediary, and Julia's exhibition of coyness in receiving his letter (I. ii); the breach in the intimacy of the lovers caused by the sending of Proteus to court; the pursuit of Proteus by Julia in disguise; Julia's lodging at an inn and overhearing Proteus' serenade to Silvia (IV. ii); the disguised Julia's taking service with Proteus as his page, and being sent by him to advance his suit to Silvia; the conversation between Julia and Silvia concerning Proteus' former love, and Silvia's rejection of his addresses (IV. iv); and Julia's final reunion with Proteus in the forest. One may add that the Felix (Proteus) of Montemayor has a conventional page who provides at least something of the rôle of Launce.

The more obvious departures of the play from the inherited story are the following: the presence of Valentine, about whom are developed the theme of manly friendship and the incidents of Proteus' treachery; the addition of Thurio, Eglamour, and Speed; the development of the rôle of the Duke as the father of Silvia; and the suppression of Celia's (Silvia's) headlong passion for the supposed boy, Felismena (Julia), and hence the elimination of Celia's voluntary death from hopeless love. These external changes, however, are far less important than the more subtle and profound departures of Shakespeare in characterization and in poetry. The superiority of the dramatist in these respects could be adequately demonstrated only through more ample and detailed comparisons than are possible here. The basis for one significant comparison may, however, be provided. Part of the most appealing conversation between Celia (Silvia) and the disguised Felismena (Julia) in the romance is recounted as follows (Yonge's translation, 1598, p. 64. Cf. Hazlitt's *Shakespeare's Library*, Part I, Vol. I, pp. 298, 299). Felismena is the speaker:

'There is not anie thing (saide *Celia*) that I would not do for thee, though I were determined not to loue him at all, who for my sake hath forsaken another. For it is no small point of wisedome for me, to learne by other womens harmes to be more wise, and warie in

mine owne. Beleeue not good Lady (saide I) that
there is any thing in the worlde, that can make *Don
Felix* forget you. And if he hath cast off another for
your sake, woonder not thereat, when your beautie and
wisedome is so great, and the others so small, that there
is no reason to thinke, that he will (though he hath
woorthelie forsaken her for your sake) or euer can
forget you for any woman else in the worlde. Doest
thou then know *Felismena* (saide *Celia*) the lady
whom thy Master did once loue and serue in his owne
countrey? I know her (saide I) although not so well
as it was needfull for me, to haue preuented so many
mishaps, (and this I spake softly to my selfe). For
my fathers house was neere to hers, but seeing your
great beautie adorned with such perfections and wisedome, *Don Felix* can not be blamed, if he hath forgotten his first loue, onely to embrace and honour
yours. To this did *Celia* answer merily, and smiling.
Thou hast learned quickly of thy Master to sooth. Not
so faire Ladie, saide I, but to serue you woulde I faine
learne: for flatterie cannot be, where (in the iudgement
of all) there are so manifest signes and proofes of this
due commendation. *Celia* began in good earnest to
aske me what manner of woman *Felismena* was; whom
I answered, that touching her beautie, Some thought
her to be very faire, but I was neuer of that opinion,
bicause she hath many daies since wanted the chiefest
thing that is requisite for it. What is that, said
Celia? Content of minde, saide I, bicause perfect
beautie can neuer be, where the same is not adioyned
to it.'

The reader who will turn from this passage to the
corresponding lines of the play (IV. iv. 125-185) may
judge of Shakespeare's achievement in delicacy and
richness of characterization, in pathos, and in poetry.

APPENDIX B

The History of the Play

We possess no text of *The Two Gentlemen of Verona* earlier than that in the First Folio of 1623, and for determining the precise date of composition we have inadequate evidence. Although the play is mentioned first, so far as we know, by Francis Meres in his *Palladis Tamia,* of 1598, certain features of style and dramatic technique indicate that it was written considerably earlier. Competent critics have proposed dates ranging between 1590 and 1595, the majority preferring the period 1591-1592. Since the extant text shows both signs of youth and characteristics which may be due to revision, we are not prohibited from surmising that Shakespeare wrote the play as early as 1590-1591, and that he or some one else made changes as late as 1594-1595. All we know for certain is that, as it stands, the play discloses bits of immature workmanship and irregularities which may arise from textual alteration.

In view of the fact that in later comedies Shakespeare improved upon virtually all features of *The Two Gentlemen of Verona,* we need not be surprised at the infrequency of stage-performances of this play. The first production of which we have a record is that by David Garrick at Drury Lane on December 22, 1762. The version presented included 'Alterations and Additions' by Benjamin Victor. Victor's literary audacity may be illustrated by his addition to the last act of two scenes designed for bringing Launce and Speed upon the stage again. The play was performed five times with success; but at the sixth performance occurred a riot motivated, apparently, partly by personal hostility to Garrick and partly by a desire for

the restoration of admission at half-price. A more
faithful presentation of Shakespeare's text occurred
at Covent Garden on April 13, 1784; and in January,
1790, John Philip Kemble gave three performances
of the original play at Drury Lane. On April 21,
1808, at Covent Garden, Kemble presented Victor's
version, with alterations of his own. Somewhat later
the play was degraded into an opera by Frederic
Reynolds, and produced at Covent Garden on November 29, 1821, and on numerous subsequent dates.
Shakespeare's own play was revived at Bath on
March 23, 1822, and at Drury Lane, by Macready,
on December 29, 1841. Charles Kean is said[1] to have
produced it both in England and in America during
the period 1840-1850, and during the following decade
Samuel Phelps gave performances at Sadler's Wells.

During recent years notable productions have been
achieved by Osmund Tearle at Stratford-upon-Avon
in 1890, by Augustin Daly in New York and London
in 1895, and by J. H. Leigh at the Court Theatre,
London, in April, 1904. In observance of the Shakespeare Tercentenary, members of the University of
Wisconsin gave two performances of the play in May,
1916.

[1] Cf. Harold Child, in *The Two Gentlemen of Verona*,
edited by Sir Arthur Quiller-Couch and John Dover Wilson
(Cambridge, 1921), p. 106. I have found no other statement
concerning these performances by Charles Kean.

APPENDIX C

The Text of the Present Edition

The earliest known text of *The Two Gentlemen of Verona* is that of the First Folio of 1623.

By permission of the Oxford University Press, the text of the present edition is that of the Oxford Shakespeare edited by W. J. Craig. Departures from Craig's text, and from that of the First Folio, are indicated below.

1. Minor changes in spelling and pronunciation have not been listed.

2. Craig's text and the present one follow the division into acts and scenes indicated in the First Folio; but the Latin designations in the Folio (e.g. *Actus primus, Scena prima*) are replaced by English equivalents.

In the First Folio the *Dramatis Personæ* ('The names of all the Actors') appear at the end of the play.

3. The stage-directions and list of *dramatis personæ* of the First Folio have been restored as far as possible, all additions being enclosed within square brackets. Aside from editorial additions within brackets, the stage-directions of the present edition differ from those of the First Folio only in the following instances, the readings of the Folio appearing after the colons:

I. iii. 91 S.d.	*Exeunt.*: *Exeunt. Finis.*	
II. iv. 215 S.d.	[*Exit.*]: *Exeunt.*	
III. i. 398 S.d.	[*Exit.*]: *Exeunt.*	
IV. iv. 212 S.d.	[*Exit.*]: *Exeunt.*	
V. ii. 7 S.d.	[*Jul. Aside.*]: *Pro.*	
13 S.d.	[*Jul. Aside.*]: *Thu.*	
56 S.d.	[*Exit.*]: *Exeunt.*	

4.   In the text of the speeches the present edition departs from the text of Craig, and restores the readings of the First Folio, in the following instances, Craig's readings appearing after the colons:

I. i. 117-119	*Speed.* [*Nodding.*] Ay.: [*Speed nods.*] Did she nod? *Speed.* Ay.
ii. 51	'fool: fool
II. iii. 20	in it: in
iv. 96	pair: pairs
197	[eye]: eye
v. 57	alehouse: alehouse so
57	an: a
III. i. 329	[kissed]: kissed
IV. iv. 6	I would: would I
92	Well,: Well, well,

5.   In the present edition, and in that of Craig, the text of the speeches departs from the text of the First Folio in the following instances, the readings of the Folio appearing after the colons:

I. i. 65	leave: love
77	a sheep: Sheepe
155	testered: cestern'd
ii. 93	your: you
iii. 88	father calls: Fathers call's
II. iii. 42	tied: tide
43	tied that ever any man tied.: Tide, that euer any man tide.
45	tied: tide
59	tied: tide
iv. 63	know: knew
109	mistress: a Mistresse
167	makes: make
197	Is it: It is
197	Valentinus': *Valentines*
v. 2	Milan: *Padua*
43	that my: that that my
III. i. 81	of Verona: in *Verona*
149	would be: should be
IV. i. 35	miserable: often miserable
49	An heir, and near: And heire and Neece,
ii. 116	his: her
iii. 17	abhors: abhor'd

iv. 61	hangman:	Hangmans
76	thou:	thee
80	to leave:	not leaue
V. ii. 32	Sir Eglamour:	*Eglamoure*
iv. 67	trusted now,:	trusted

APPENDIX D

SUGGESTIONS FOR COLLATERAL READING

William Hazlitt: *Characters of Shakespear's Plays* (1817). (Reprinted in Everyman's Library. See pp. 203-205.)

W. C. Hazlitt: *Shakespeare's Library,* Part I, Vol. I (London, 1875), pp. 275-312. (Reprint of the story of Felix and Felismena from Bartholomew Yonge's translation of Montemayor's *Diana.* See above, pp. 90-92.)

Grace Latham: *On Julia, Silvia, Hero and Viola,* in *Transactions of the New Shakspere Society,* 1887-1892, Part IV, pp. 319-350.

Andrew Lang: *The Comedies of Shakespeare.* With illustrations by E. A. Abbey. XI. *Two Gentlemen of Verona.* Harper's New Monthly Magazine, December, 1894, vol. LXXXVIII, pp. 134-147.

Lewis Lewes: *The Women of Shakespeare* (New York and London, 1895), pp. 137-140.

The Two Gentlemen of Verona (The Arden Edition), edited by R. Warwick Bond (London, 1906).

G. P. Baker: *The Development of Shakespeare as a Dramatist* (New York, 1907), pp. 116-123.

A. H. Tolman: *Questions on Shakespeare,* Part II (Chicago, [1910]), pp. 261-297.

Brander Matthews: *Shakspere as a Playwright* (New York, 1913), pp. 73-78.

The Two Gentlemen of Verona, edited by Sir Arthur Quiller-Couch and John Dover Wilson (Cambridge, 1921).

R. M. Alden: *Shakespeare* (New York, 1922), pp. 200-203.

INDEX OF WORDS GLOSSED

(Figures in full-faced type refer to page-numbers)

A B C: 16 (II. i. 24)
advice: 32 (II. iv. 208, 209);
42 (III. i. 73)
again: 20 (II. i. 129)
again reply (reply): 21 (II.
i. 174)
agood: 72 (IV. iv. 172)
aim (noun): 41 (III. i. 28)
aim to, give: 81 (V. iv. 101)
aimed at: 41 (III. i. 45)
air, live in your: 26 (II. iv.
28)
ale: 35 (II. v. 62)
all one: 49 (III. i. 264)
allycholly: 61 (IV. ii. 28)
alone: 31 (II. iv. 168)
angerly: 9 (I. ii. 60)
an (prep.): 69 (IV. iv. 68)
an if: 3 (I. i. 75)
another, such: 44 (III. i.
133)
anthem: 48 (III. i. 241)
any length, of: 44 (III. i.
130)
anything to take to: 58 (IV.
i. 42)
apparent: 44 (III. i. 116)
approach (noun): 78 (V. iv.
31)
approved: 79 (V. iv. 43)
arms' end: 79 (V. iv. 57)
as: 11 (I. ii. 107)
attend on: 46 (III. i. 186)
awful: 58 (IV. i. 46)

baa: 4 (I. i. 98)
back, give: 82 (V. iv. 126)
bare: 49 (III. i. 273)
base: 10 (I. ii. 94)
be in eye of: 13 (I. iii. 32)
beadsman: 1 (I. i. 18)

befortune: 66 (IV. iii. 41)
beholding: 72 (IV. iv. 180)
belike: 28 (II. iv. 91)
beshrew: 5 (I. i. 134)
bestow: 43 (III. i. 87)
bid the base: 10 (I. ii. 94)
black: 43 (III. i. 103)
bless the mark: 67 (IV. iv.
21)
blood: 44 (III. i. 121)
blow (verb): 2 (I. i. 46)
blunt: 36 (II. vi. 41)
boots (verb): 2 (I. i. 28)
boots, give me not the: 2 (I.
i. 27)
bottom (verb): 55 (III. ii.
53)
break with: 13 (I. iii. 44)
break with . . . of: 42 (III.
i. 59)
bring: 3 (I. i. 55)
broker: 8 (I. ii. 39)
brook (verb): 77 (V. iii. 4)
burden (noun): 10 (I. ii.
82)
by a figure: 21 (II. i. 156)

calm (adj.): 79 (V. iv. 42)
canker: 2 (I. i. 43)
censure (verb): 7 (I. ii. 19)
change (noun): 62 (IV. ii.
69)
charactered: 37 (II. vii. 4)
circumstance (state of affairs): 2 (I. i. 37); (circumlocution): 2 (I. i.
36); (detailed proof): 4
(I. i. 84); (much detail):
54 (III. ii. 36)
cite: 28 (II. iv. 86)
clerkly: 19 (II. i. 119)

close (noun): **82** (V. iv. 117)

closed: **33** (II. v. 13)

cod-piece: **38** (II. vii. 53)

coil: **10** (I. ii. 96)

cold: **73** (IV. iv. 188)

colour (noun): **60** (IV. ii. 3)

commend (commit): **1** (I. i. 17); **13** (I. iii. 42); (deliver): **60** (IV. ii. 9)

commendations (greetings): **14** (I. iii. 53)

commended, them much (sent kind greetings): **29** (II. iv. 124)

commit: **80** (V. iv. 77)

common: **80** (V. iv. 62)

compass (verb): **33** (II. iv. 215)

competitor: **36** (II. vi. 35)

conceit: **54** (III. ii. 17)

conceitless: **63** (IV. ii. 99)

concerns (verb): **9** (I. ii. 74)

condition: **49** (III. i. 275)

conditions, on such slight: **82** (V. iv. 138)

consort (company of musicians): **56** (III. ii. 84); (fellowship): **59** (IV. i. 64)

conversed: **27** (II. iv. 64)

correction: **53** (III. i. 398)

counts of: **18** (II. i. 67)

crystal looks, locked in her: **28** (II. iv. 90)

cry you mercy: **81** (V. iv. 94)

curst: **52** (III. i. 350)

dear: **65** (IV. iii. 14)

deign: **6** (I. i. 162)

delight, pageants of: **72** (IV. iv. 166)

delivered: **69** (IV. iv. 79)

derived: **75** (V. ii. 23)

descant: **10** (I. ii. 91)

desert (noun): **77** (V. iv. 2)

desperate: **53** (III. ii. 5)

die on: **29** (II. iv. 115)

dined: **21** (II. i. 179)

discipline: **56** (III. ii. 88)

discover: **40** (III. i. 4); **56** (III. ii. 77)

discovery: **41** (III. i. 45)

dispose: **39** (II. vii. 86)

dog at, a: **67** (IV. iv. 14)

doublet: **26** (II. iv. 20)

drier death on shore: **6** (I. i. 160)

drift (noun): **36** (II. vi. 43); **40** (III. i. 18); **63** (IV. ii. 84)

ducat: **6** (I. i. 147)

dump (noun): **56** (III. ii. 85)

earnest (noun): **21** (II. i. 165)

else: **64** (IV. ii. 127)

emperor: **13** (I. iii. 27)

encounters (noun): **38** (II. vii. 41)

end, arms': **79** (V. iv. 57)

end, still an: **69** (IV. iv. 68)

enfranchised: **28** (II. iv. 91)

engine: **44** (III. i. 138)

entertain: **29** (II. iv. 105); **69** (IV. iv. 76)

Eve's legacy: **51** (III. i. 345)

except against: **15** (I. iii. 83); **31** (II. iv. 156)

exceptions, take: **15** (I. iii. 81); **75** (V. ii. 3)

excuse (verb): **14** (I. iii. 71)

exhibition: **14** (I. iii. 69)

expostulate: **48** (III. i. 252)

eye of, be in: **13** (I. iii. 32)

fain: **5** (I. i. 128)

fair: **75** (V. ii. 9)

fancy (noun): **42** (III. i. 67)

fantastic: **38** (II. vii. 47)

farthingale: **38** (II. vii. 51)

favour (noun): **17** (II. i. 62)

feature: **28** (II. iv. 74)

figure, by a: **21** (II. i. 156)

flat: **10** (I. ii. 90)

fond: **3** (I. i. 52)

fool, poor: **70** (IV. iv. 100)

'fool: **8** (I. ii. 51)

for (because): **31** (II. iv. 176); **66** (IV. iii. 24)

for (for fear of): **12** (I. ii. 133)

for why: **43** (III. i. 99)

forgot: **43** (III. i. 85)

forth: **32** (II. iv. 187)

fortuned: **83** (V. iv. 169)

friar: **58** (IV. i. 36)

gave aim to: **81** (V. iv. 101)

'give: **19** (II. i. 108)

give back: **82** (V. iv. 126)

give leave: **40** (III. i. 1)

give me not the boots: **2** (I. i. 27)

give the onset to: **56** (III. ii. 94)

go: **60** (IV. ii. 20)

go to: **16** (II. i. 15)

go to it: **67** (IV. iv. 5)

go to the ale: **35** (II. v. 62)

go ungartered: **18** (II. i. 81)

gossips: **49** (III. i. 270)

grace (noun): **45** (III. i. 146)

graced: **14** (I. iii. 58)

gracious: **53** (III. i. 381)

grievance (grieving): **56** (III. ii. 86)

grievances (distresses): **66** (IV. iii. 37)

grievously: **54** (III. ii. 14)

habit: **81** (V. iv. 104)

halidom: **64** (IV. ii. 138)

Hallowmas: **16** (II. i. 28)

hammering: **12** (I. iii. 18)

hangman (adj.): **69** (IV. iv. 61)

haply: **1** (I. i. 12)

happy messenger: **27** (II. iv. 54)

harbour (verb): **44** (III. i. 140)

hard-favoured: **17** (II. i. 55)

have: **78** (V. iv. 15)

heat: **32** (II. iv. 193)

heavy: **10** (I. ii. 81)

herald (adj.): **45** (III. i. 144)

Hero: **44** (III. i. 119)

horns: **4** (I. i. 79)

horse: **49** (III. i. 266)

hose, round: **38** (II. vii. 55)

how sayest thou: **34** (II. v. 43)

however: **2** (I. i. 34)

ill-favoured: **38** (II. vii. 54)

impeachment: **12** (I. iii. 15)

imperial (noun): **23** (II. iii. 5)

importune (urge): **12** (I. iii. 13)

importune (command): **45** (III. i. 145)

impose (noun): **65** (IV. iii. 8)

imprimis: **49** (III. i. 275)

in eye of: **13** (I. iii. 32)

in good time: **13** (I. iii. 44)

in print, speak: **21** (II. i. 177)

in telling: **6** (I. i. 150)

include: **83** (V. iv. 160)

indifferent: **55** (III. ii. 44)

infinite (noun): **39** (II. vii. 70)

influence (noun): **46** (III. i. 183)

inhabit: **2** (I. i. 44); **61** (IV. ii. 49); **78** (V. iv. 7)
inherit: **56** (III. ii. 87)
inly: **37** (II. vii. 18)
integrity: **56** (III. ii. 77)
interpret: **19** (II. i. 105)
is privilege for: **45** (III. i. 160)

jade: **49** (III. i. 278)
jars (noun): **83** (V. iv. 160)
jerkin: **26** (II. iv. 20)
jolthead: **50** (III. i. 292)

keep: **67** (IV. iv. 12)
kept withal: **83** (V. iv. 152)
kill: **9** (I. ii. 66)
kind (kindred): **23** (II. iii. 2)
kind (nature): **43** (III. i. 90)
knave, one: **49** (III. i. 264)

laced mutton: **4** (I. i. 102)
Leander: **2** (I. i. 22); **44** (III. i. 120)
learn: **35** (II. vi. 13); **77** (V. iii. 4)
lease, out by: **76** (V. ii. 29)
leave (cease): **35** (II. vi. 17)
leave (part with): **69** (IV. iv. 80)
leave, give: **40** (III. i. 1)
legacy, Eve's: **51** (III. i. 345)
length, of any: **44** (III. i. 130)
lets: **44** (III. i. 113)
liberal: **52** (III. i. 357)
lies (verb): **64** (IV. ii. 139)
lightly: **45** (III. i. 142)
Light o' Love: **10** (I. ii. 80)
likes: **62** (IV. ii. 56)
lime: **55** (III. ii. 68)
lions, one of the: **16** (II. i. 30)

live in your air: **26** (II. iv. 28)
locked in her crystal looks: **28** (II. iv. 90)
loiterer: **50** (III. i. 298)
longing (adj.): **39** (II. vii. 85)
love-book: **1** (I. i. 19)
lumpish: **55** (III. ii. 62)

makes it strange: **10** (I. ii. 99)
manage: **48** (III. i. 248)
mark, bless the: **67** (IV. iv. 21)
marry (interjection): **5** (I. i. 131)
me ('ethical dative'): **67** (IV. iv. 10)
mean (musical term): **10** (I. ii. 92)
means (efforts): **82** (V. iv. 137)
measure (noun): **82** (V. iv. 127)
meat: **9** (I. ii. 66)
meed: **29** (II. iv. 113)
mercy, cry you: **81** (V. iv. 94)
Merops: **45** (III. i. 153)
messenger: **27** (II. iv. 54)
month's mind: **12** (I. ii. 134)
mood: **59** (IV. i. 51)
more hair than wit: **52** (III. i. 363)
motion: **19** (II. i. 104)
mountain-foot: **76** (V. ii. 46)
mouth, sweet: **51** (III. i. 333)
moved: **8** (I. ii. 27)
muse (verb): **14** (I. iii. 64)
mutton: **4** (I. i. 102)

nameless: **51** (III. i. 322)
nice: **42** (III. i. 82)

Nicholas, Saint: 50 (III. i. 303)

nick, out of all: 62 (IV. ii. 77)

no reason but: 32 (II. iv. 213)

noddy: 5 (I. i. 120)

of: 67 (IV. iv. 3)

of any length: 44 (III. i. 130)

omitting: 27 (II. iv. 66)

on: 15 (II. i. 1)

on, attend: 46 (III. i. 186)

on such slight conditions: 82 (V. iv. 138)

one: 15 (II. i. 2)

one knave: 49 (III. i. 264)

one of the lions: 16 (II. i. 30)

onset, give the: 56 (III. ii. 94)

on such slight conditions: 82 (V. iv. 138)

open (verb): 5 (I. i. 137)

out by lease: 76 (V. ii. 29)

out of all nick: 62 (IV. ii. 77)

overcharged: 4 (I. i. 107)

overlooked: 8 (I. ii. 48)

owe: 75 (V. ii. 28)

pageants of delight: 72 (IV. iv. 166)

pardon (verb): 57 (III. ii. 98)

parle: 7 (I. ii. 5)

passenger: 57 (IV. i. 1)

passing: 7 (I. ii. 17)

passioning: 72 (IV. iv. 174)

pawn (noun): 13 (I. iii. 47)

pearls: 75 (V. ii. 13)

peasant: 76 (V. ii. 35)

peevish: 76 (V. ii. 49)

Pentecost: 72 (IV. iv. 165)

perceive: 6 (I. i. 146)

peremptory: 14 (I. iii. 71)

period: 20 (II. i. 127)

Phaethon: 45 (III. i. 153)

picture: 32 (II. iv. 210)

pinfold: 5 (I. i. 114)

plead: 82 (V. iv. 144)

poor fool: 70 (IV. iv. 100)

possessions: 75 (V. ii. 25)

post (noun): 6 (I. i. 163)

postern: 74 (V. i. 9)

pound (verb): 5 (I. i. 110)

practising: 59 (IV. i. 48)

praise (verb): 52 (III. i. 353)

prefer: 31 (II. iv. 158)

presently: 9 (I. ii. 57)

pretence: 41 (III. i. 47)

pretended: 36 (II. vi. 37)

prime: 2 (I. i. 49)

principality: 30 (II. iv. 153)

print (noun): 21 (II. i. 177)

privilege for, is: 45 (III. i. 160)

prodigious: 23 (II. iii. 4)

proper: 57 (IV. i. 10)

proportion: 23 (II. iii. 3)

protestation: 10 (I. ii. 96)

provided: 14 (I. iii. 72)

puddings: 68 (IV. iv. 34)

puling: 16 (II. i. 27)

puppet: 19 (II. i. 105)

quaintly: 20 (II. i. 133); 44 (III. i. 117)

quality: 59 (IV. i. 58)

quips: 60 (IV. ii. 12)

quote: 26 (II. iv. 18)

ravel: 55 (III. ii. 52)

reason (noun): 32 (II. iv. 213)

reasoning (verb): 20 (II. i. 151)

receive: 80 (V. iv. 78)

record (verb): 78 (V. iv. 6)

recover: 74 (V. i. 12)

relish (verb): 16 (II. i. 21)

remorseful: 65 (IV. iii. 13)

repeal (verb): **48** (III. i. 235); **82** (V. iv. 143)

reply, again (verb): **21** (II. i. 174)

resort (noun): **7** (I. ii. 4)

respect (prize): **11** (I. ii. 131)

respect (heed): **43** (III. i. 89); **78** (V. iv. 20)

respects (takes into account): **79** (V. iv. 54)

respective: **73** (IV. iv. 202)

rest (noun): **59** (IV. i. 60)

road: **3** (I. i. 53); **32** (II. iv. 188)

root: **81** (V. iv. 103)

round hose: **38** (II. vii. 55)

sad: **12** (I. iii. 1)

Saint Nicholas: **50** (III. i. 303)

scandalized: **38** (II. vii. 61)

search (verb): **11** (I. ii. 113)

senseless: **45** (III. i. 143)

servant: **19** (II. i. 110)

serviceable: **56** (III. ii. 70)

set (musical term): **9** (I. ii. 78)

set (seated): **18** (II. i. 95)

set the world on wheels: **51** (III. i. 320)

shadow (portrait): **64** (IV. ii. 128); **73** (IV. iv. 204)

shadow (lifeless person): **64** (IV. ii. 127); **73** (IV. iv. 204)

shadow (illusion): **46** (III. i. 177)

shapeless: **1** (I. i. 8)

shipped: **3** (I. i. 54, 72)

shot (noun): **33** (II. v. 7)

silly: **59** (IV. i. 72)

sinews: **56** (III. ii. 78)

sirrah: **16** (II. i. 8)

slow: **62** (IV. ii. 66)

so: **44** (III. i. 120)

soho: **46** (III. i. 189)

solemnity: **83** (V. iv. 161)

something (rather, somewhat): **14** (I. iii. 63)

sort (verb): **56** (III. ii. 92)

sorted: **14** (I. iii. 63)

speak in print: **21** (II. i. 177)

speed (verb): **70** (IV. iv. 114)

squirrel: **69** (IV. iv. 60)

state (noun): **82** (V. iv. 144)

stays (verb): **11** (I. ii. 128)

stead: **19** (II. i. 124)

stick (verb): **4** (I. i. 108)

still: **1** (I. i. 9)

still an end: **69** (IV. iv. 68)

still approved: **79** (V. iv. 43)

stock (stocking): **50** (III. i. 315)

stock (dowry): **50** (III. i. 314)

stomach: **9** (I. ii. 66)

stones: **6** (I. i. 151)

strange: **10** (I. ii. 99)

subtle: **63** (IV. ii. 98)

success: **3** (I. i. 58)

such another: **44** (III. i. 133)

suggested: **41** (III. i. 34)

sure: **74** (V. i. 12)

swain: **78** (V. iv. 12)

sweet mouth: **51** (III. i. 333)

sweet-suggesting: **35** (II. vi. 7)

swinged: **18** (II. i. 91)

table: **37** (II. vii. 3)

take exceptions: **15** (I. iii. 81); **75** (V. ii. 3)

take to, anything to: **58** (IV. i. 42)

take up (rebuke): **11** (I. ii. 132)

take up (oppose): **73** (IV. iv. 204)

tangle: **55** (III. ii. 68)

tarriance: **39** (II. vii. 90)

temper (verb): **55** (III. ii. 64)

tender (verb): **71** (IV. iv. 147)

tender (adj.): **79** (V. iv. 37)

testerned: **6** (I. i. 155)

testy: **9** (I. ii. 56)

that (so that): **16** (II. i. 33); **43** (III. i. 109, 112)

though: **48** (III. i. 256)

thought (noun): **3** (I. i. 69)

throughly: **11** (I. ii. 112)

tide: **22** (II. ii. 14); **24** (II. iii. 40)

time, in good: **13** (I. iii. 44)

time, of greater: **38** (II. vii. 48)

timeless: **40** (III. i. 21)

tire (noun): **73** (IV. iv. 192)

to: **30** (II. iv. 139)

to it, go: **67** (IV. iv. 5)

tongues: **58** (IV. i. 33)

trenched: **53** (III. ii. 7)

trencher: **67** (IV. iv. 10)

trimmed: **72** (IV. iv. 168)

triumphs (noun): **83** (V. iv. 161)

turn (verb): **22** (II. ii. 4)

turn (noun): **44** (III. i. 131)

unadvised: **71** (IV. iv. 129)

ungartered, go: **18** (II. i. 81)

unmellowed: **27** (II. iv. 71)

unstaid: **38** (II. vii. 60)

up and down: **24** (II. iii. 32)

urinal: **17** (II. i. 43)

Valentine: **46** (III. i. 192, 193)

very (adj.): **55** (III. ii. 41)

wasps: **10** (I. ii. 103)

watch (verb): **16** (II. i. 26); **65** (IV. ii. 143)

water-spaniel: **49** (III. i. 273)

well-favoured: **17** (II. i. 56)

went to it: **67** (IV. iv. 5)

wheels, set the world on: **51** (III. i. 320)

where: **42** (III. i. 74)

whoreson: **68** (IV. iv. 48)

why, for: **43** (III. i. 99)

wink: **12** (I. ii. 136)

withal: **39** (II. vii. 67)

withal, kept: **83** (V. iv. 152)

wood (adj.): **24** (II. iii. 31)

wot: **68** (IV. iv. 31)

wreathe: **16** (II. i. 20)